The Great Commission Alliance
7015 Casa Elena Dr. NE
Albuquerque, NM 87113

www.greatcommissionalliance.org

To Dad.

Thank you for loving God, loving me, and showing me how to love and cherish God and His Word. Thank you for boldly following the Lord and sharing your faith, and teaching me to as well. Your example inspires and motivates me. Neither the ministry I am privileged to be a part of, nor this book would ever have happened without you. I thank God for you and love you a ton Dad.

Special thanks to:

Meghan Renfro for doing an amazing job with the graphic design.

Erin Herbst, Brandon and Anne Cox, Joan Ross, and Emray and Carol Goosen for your contributions.

The Lighthouse Foundation and GCA team who live out the truths in this devotional, and teach others to do the same each and every day.

Our amazing ministry supporters, without whom we couldn't do what we do.

Contents

Romans 1:16

For I am not ashamed of the gospel,
because it is the power of God for
salvation to everyone who believes,
first to the Jew, and also to the Greek.

FOREWORD

"You will be my witnesses to...the ends of the earth." These words, recorded in Acts 1:8, were the last words Jesus spoke on this earth. Then He rose bodily into the clouds as his disciples looked on! Jesus' words echo down the corridors of eternity and are the spark in every true believer's heart.

Do you want to make an impact for Christ? If so, this short devotional is an excellent place to start. Each day will begin with a short passage from Scripture that will encourage you in the area of personal evangelism.

In my continuing encounters with pastors and Christian leaders all over the world, I find that I never need to "sell" personal evangelism to them. They know that God has enlisted us all in this Great Commission! They know! It's inside them! They know that we truly are all "workers together with God," "ambassadors," and "fellow laborers" empowered by the Holy Spirit Himself to do and to finish His Great Commission!

They know!

They are simply looking for a workable way to train and mobilize the people they lead!

This is where Nate Herbst and the Great Commission Alliance come in! Nate and his team travel to the world's nations delivering a practical, relational, and transferable method of personal evangelism to Christ's leaders around the globe. The pastors, in turn, multiply it with their changed lifestyle, and then by passing this practical and powerful training on to those they lead! It becomes a refreshing new lifestyle! A "new normal!" The results have been thousands coming to Christ, churches growing, and new churches being multiplied to "the ends of the earth."

I invite you to let this day-by-day devotional be a regular part of the time you spend with your Savior every day. I guarantee that adding these reflections to your daily times with Jesus will refresh you, renew you, and change your life! You will be inspired at first, but after a few weeks, you'll notice a wonderful "new normal" happening in your life too! Your heart will cry out to God, "Lord, I'm available today to touch someone's life with my witness of You." The most exciting thing is that God will answer your prayer!

May you be blessed in your journeys in this life, and may you be enriched and equipped with all you need to fulfill your God-ordained destiny on this earth! Then we'll meet in heaven someday!

Darrell Dobbelmann
President of Dove International
Evangelist with Oasis World Ministries

INTRODUCTION

Thank you for picking up this little devotional. God created you for a life of impact, and I believe He will use this little devotional to encourage you tremendously in all He has for you. Get ready for an incredible journey!

Evangelism can be a scary topic. Many of us deal with fear when it comes to sharing our faith. I sure do! I've also found a life of adventure and significance on the other side of that fear. I know you will too.

Let me tell you a short story. Several years ago, I took my wife on a surprise trip to Hawaii for our fifth anniversary. It was amazing. On that trip, we did a little snorkeling, something I had never done before. Although Erin got the hang of it immediately, I struggled with it. I couldn't bring myself to breathe with my face underwater. I kept hyperventilating and splashing around like I was getting attacked by a shark.

I was absolutely miserable for the first thirty or forty minutes of trying. I'm thankful I persevered. Once I got the hang of breathing with my face underwater, I was stunned by the beauty just below the waves. There were stunning formations and fish of every kind and color swimming all around me. If I hadn't persevered through the difficulty, I never would have experienced this incredible adventure.

It is exactly the same with evangelism. God has invited you and me to join Him in His work. He has empowered us with His Spirit. Joining Him in what He is doing is undoubtedly one of the greatest things anyone could ever experience. Still, so many let their fears and failures keep them from all God has for them.

I want to ask you to take a big step of faith and to trust God to do something special in your life over the next thirty-one days. You will be challenged as you go through this devotional. Some of it will make you uncomfortable. Please, stick with it and allow God to use it in a mighty way in your life.

If you will commit to working through this devotional as you walk with the Lord over the next month, I believe you will be a radically different person by the time you finish it. As you dive into God's word each day, you will find a life of meaning and significance you may have never imagined possible.

God has a great plan for you. My hope and prayer is that this little devotional will equip you for that purpose. Thanks again for getting this book. I hope and pray God uses it in a special way in your life.

Nate Herbst
December, 2018

— DAY —
ONE

Matthew 28:18-20

Jesus came near and said to them, "All authority has been given to me in heaven and on earth. Go, therefore, and make disciples of all nations, baptizing them in the name of the Father and of the Son and of the Holy Spirit, teaching them to observe everything I have commanded you. And remember, I am with you always, to the end of the age."

Hundreds of people will die by the time you are finished with this morning's devotional. In fact, more than 150,000 will die today, and most of them will enter an eternity apart from Jesus. We don't have the luxury of complacency. The world needs Jesus, and we are His plan for reaching them.

In today's passage, we read some of the last words spoken by Jesus before He returned to the Father. The importance of this instruction, the Great Commission, cannot be overstated. In these verses, Jesus asserts His preeminence, defines our purpose, and leaves us with an incredible promise.

JESUS' PREEMINENCE

Jesus reminds His disciples that all authority in heaven and on earth is His. He is our Lord, Savior, and God (Matthew 1:23, John 1:1, 8:58, 20:28, Philippians 2:6, and 2 Peter 1:11). Those who love and follow Him will obey Him (John 14:15 and 15:14). He is our preeminent Lord, and all authority is His; we cannot refuse Him. We must, out of our love for Him, walk in the purpose He calls us to.

OUR PURPOSE

Christ's parting command to His followers was to make disciples. This pattern of spiritual multiplication, outlined further by Paul in 2 Timothy 2:2, is simple, strategic, and staggeringly effective. This plan is for all believers, it encompasses all of the world, and it will have an impact on all of eternity. Following this protocol, Jesus' disciples saw a huge percentage of the known world of their day reached during their lifetimes. With this strategy, we could see the rest won in ours.

Imagine you were the only believer alive but committed to this process of making disciples and multiplying once annually, teaching those you reached to do the same. The whole world would be reached in less than four decades! If the billion or more believers alive today began doing this, the Great Commission would be completed in just a few years. This isn't just a great plan, it is Christ's command for reaching this world, and He has promised to walk with us as we follow Him and make disciples.

AN INCREDIBLE PROMISE

Jesus concludes His Great Commission with a great promise, telling us that He will be with us always, to the end of the age. As we step out with a commitment to do the work He has called us to, we do it with the confidence that He will be with us every step of the way. No challenge, obstacle, fear, or insecurity can compete with Him, and He will never leave us (Hebrews 13:5).

"Never underestimate the power of multiplication to fulfill the Great Commission. When you totally commit yourself to a life of radical discipleship and making disciples, you can unleash an unstoppable force ... If you want to make a huge impact, implement the power of multiplication." - Dave Early

---

If you have trusted Christ as Savior and Lord, He has called you to reach others for Him and to make disciples who will continue that process until the Great Commission is completed. You don't have what it takes but your preeminent Savior does, and He has promised to enable you for this purpose.

MAKING AN IMPACT

When Isaiah heard God's call, he enthusiastically responded, "Here I am. Send me" (Isaiah 6:8). This devotional will challenge you. Before going any further, please decide how you will respond.

☐ God, here I am; change me, use me, and send me.

☐ I'm calling it quits now to maintain the status quo.

DAY
TWO

Acts 17:26-27

From one man He has made every nationality to live over the whole earth and has determined their appointed times and the boundaries of where they live. He did this so that they might seek God, and perhaps they might reach out and find Him, though He is not far from each one of us.

In the summer of 2012, Erin and I were driving up the coast of California. We had a very hard time finding a hotel and finally found one we weren't excited about in a city we had not planned to stop in. That night, as I checked in to the hotel, I asked the hotel receptionist what the church scene was like in the city. He responded that he felt terrible about not being able to go to church because his work schedule wouldn't allow it. That opened up into a conversation about the Gospel. After an hour of talking, he decided to believe in Jesus as Savior and Lord. The next morning a fellow guest did too. This is one of my favorite stories because it illustrates the reality that God is strategically aligning the details of our lives for His purposes. We each must decide if we will join Him in what He is doing all around us.

Paul spoke the words in today's passage on a hill below the Acropolis in Athens. He shared this in the context of his evangelistic message to the Athenians. The truths he states in these two verses should not be forgotten by any believer who wants to make an impact for Christ. In this passage, Paul reminds us of God's plan, our role, and a global harvest.

GOD'S PLAN

The same God who sovereignly designed the universe and this planet has engineered the times and the places of its inhabitants so that they might find Him. Where you live, work, shop, and travel are not an accident. Neither is the time that you are alive. God has intentionally placed you in a specific place at a specific time so that those in your sphere of influence will have the opportunity to find Him through you. Jesus came to seek and to save the lost (Luke 19:10). He is continuing that mission through you and me today. God has a great plan, and He has a role for you in it.

YOUR ROLE

You are not an accident. You are His masterpiece created for an important role in His plan for the world (Ephesians 2:10). Every minute is important. Every circumstance is significant. Every relationship matters. Every interaction is an opportunity. We are each surrounded by divinely strategized circumstances that permeate each and every day. The question we must answer is whether we will make the most of those opportunities (Colossians 4:5). There is a harvest going on all around us, and we have been invited by our Lord to join Him in all that He is doing.

A GLOBAL HARVEST

There has never been a more exciting time to be alive. God has strategically placed people where they will be best reached, and transportation, communication, and many other technological advances have made reaching them for Christ more possible today than ever before. Tens of thousands of people are putting their trust in Christ each and every day. The harvest is incredibly plentiful, but the workers are still too few (Matthew 9:36-38). Now is the time for believers everywhere to join the Lord in His great harvest!

> "Christ's plan for my day and my time
> trumps my plan." - Hugh Ross

God has a great plan, and He has designed you for a special role in His global harvest. Will you join Him in what He is doing all around you?

MAKING AN IMPACT

God has strategically placed you where you are for this very time. Every place you go, thing you do, and situation you are involved in is an opportunity. Ask the Lord to highlight the circumstances that He has been setting up all around you. Ask Him what He would have you do in each of these occurrences. Write down any steps He conveys below.

_____

_____

_____

_____

THREE

Ephesians 2:10 (NLT)

For we are God's masterpiece. He has created us anew in Christ Jesus, so that we can do the good things he planned for us long ago.

Most of us deal with insecurities and self-doubt. If you have ever questioned your capacity for the life of meaning, purpose, and impact God has called you to, you are not alone. Remember Moses? He doubted himself, his calling, his ability, and his eloquence, and he begged God to send someone else instead (Exodus 3:11-4:17). If you can relate, the message in today's passage is for you!

This little passage in Ephesians reminds us of our Master, the fact that we are His masterpieces, and the reality of the mission He has prepared us for. Whatever your doubts or insecurities, He wants to use you in great ways!

THE MASTER

It is no surprise that this passage starts by reminding us that we are His. He is our Master, and until we get that piece figured out the puzzle will never make sense. We don't do what we do for any other reason than because of Him. He is the one who has made you, designed you, and prepared you for a very special part in His work (Psalm 100:3, 139:1-18, Romans 12:4-8, and 1 Corinthians 12:12-27). It is only in and through Him that you will ever be able to do what He has prepared you for (John 15:5). Because of Him, you can have confidence in who He has made you to be.

THE MASTERPIECE

The mind-boggling reality is that in Him you are a masterpiece. By grace and through faith, you have been made new (Ephesians 2:8-9). You might not feel like it, but you are. God has a proven track record of turning failures into masterpieces. Abraham doubted God's ability to do what He had promised, but God called him faithful (Romans

4:18-24). Rahab was a prostitute whose life was redeemed and whose descendants included both King David and Jesus (Matthew 1:5). David committed adultery and murder, but God called him a man after His own heart (Acts 13:22). Paul persecuted Christians, but God transformed him into an unparalleled leader (1 Corinthians 15:9). However regrettable your past, you were transformed by Jesus when you put your faith in Him (1 Corinthians 6:8-11). In Him, you are a new creation (2 Corinthians 5:17). As a new creation, you have an important mission.

THE MISSION

We are the Master's masterpieces, and we have been created for a mission, the good works He has prepared for us. Jesus came to seek and to save the lost (Luke 19:10). It is a privilege to join Him in that same mission today. God wants us to shine brightly for Him (Matthew 5:14-16). We are called to live Christ-like lives so others will see Him in us (1 Peter 2:12). We also must preach the Gospel because people need to hear the Good News in order to be saved (Romans 10:13-15). Ultimately, our mission is the Great Commission (Matthew 28:18-20). Our lives, deeds, and words should all revolve around our Master and the mission He has given us.

"I'm just a nobody trying to tell everybody, about somebody, who can save anybody." - Lyrics From a Williams Brothers song

Your Master has made you a masterpiece for an important mission. Don't let your fears, insecurities, or doubts be excuses for not experiencing the life of meaning and purpose God has prepared for you. Whatever you feel about yourself, remember the truth of who you are in Him. Step out in that today, walking closely with the Master, and watch Him use you in spite of your weaknesses and limitations.

MAKING AN IMPACT

What fears and insecurities paralyze you when it comes to the mission God has called you to? Ask God to reveal these to you. Write down anything He makes you aware of below. Then, draw a big X through them and decide today to trust Him with these limitations.

Matthew 9:36-38

When He saw the crowds, He felt compassion for them, because they were distressed and dejected, like sheep without a shepherd. Then He said to His disciples, "The harvest is abundant, but the workers are few. Therefore, pray to the Lord of the harvest to send out workers into His harvest."

Getting stuck in our own little Christian bubble is easy. We often look at the world with the impression that it's lost and beyond hope, that it is somehow worse now than it ever has been before. We see the news and hear the statistics and often react by retreating into our Christian safe zones and distancing ourselves from the lost. If you are comfortable where you are at, you won't want anything to do with today's passage.

Jesus' words in these short verses are absolutely paradigm changing. What He demonstrates and communicates here cultivates compassion, clarifies comprehension, and challenges commitment.

COMPASSION

Jesus looked at the crowds with compassion, recognizing they were "distressed and dejected, like sheep without a shepherd." It is easy to believe the lie that people are happy and satisfied the way they are. There is a modern epidemic of depression, stress, anxiety, addictions, broken relationships, and loneliness. Even the few that have managed to elude these ills are empty without Christ. Many are also heading toward an eternity apart from Him. The truth is that the world needs Jesus desperately. Jesus knew this and responded with compassion. We need to see them the same way. That requires a change in our comprehension.

COMPREHENSION

It is easy to look at the depravity of the world and assume that the lost are uninterested and unreachable. Instead of being bright lights for

Jesus we often resort to complaining about the darkness. Many of us believe our society is the biggest impediment to the Gospel. Nothing could be further from the truth. According to Jesus, believers are the limiting factor in the harvest. The insanity you see in the world is just evidence of empty people trying desperately to be satisfied. Jesus is the only solution, and they need Him today as much as ever. People are no different today than ever before. They are still just sinners looking for a Savior. The truth is that the limiting factor in the harvest has always been the workers! It's time we commit to serving Him in His harvest.

COMMITMENT

Jesus tells us the harvest is ripe. No sane farmer would sit idly by during harvest time. There has never been a time in human history when more people were alive and searching than today. It is an unbelievable privilege to be here at this time for this unparalleled opportunity. God is not willing that any would perish and He wants everyone to come to know Him (2 Peter 3:9 and 1 Timothy 2:4). That has always been His desire (Genesis 12:1-3, Psalm 22:27, and Matthew 28:18-20). The harvest is very abundant, but the workers are few. Knowing this challenges us to commit to the Lord and His work.

I am. - G. K. Chesterton's Chesterton's full essay for a national competition on what was wrong with the world.

The harvest is abundant, but the workers are few. That is the truth. No harvest can harvest itself, and without harvesters, it can't help but rot in the field. The problem isn't with the harvest but with the lack of harvesters. We need to share Christ's compassion, adjust our comprehension, and renew our commitment to Him and the impact He has called us to.

MAKING AN IMPACT

Jesus' answer in this passage is to pray. Remember, we can do nothing apart from Him (John 15:5). Take a minute now to ask the Lord to give you His heart for the lost. Spend a few minutes praying for lost friends. Then, make yourself available to be used just as Jesus' disciples were immediately after Jesus spoke these words to them (see Matthew Chapter 10). Ask God how He would use you and write down whatever He prompts.

---

FIVE

2 Peter 3:9 (NLT)

The Lord isn't really being slow about his promise to return, as some people think. No, He is being patient for your sake. He does not want anyone to perish, so He is giving more time for everyone to repent.

Here is an encouraging truth to start your day out with: God doesn't want anyone to perish! However shellshocked we might feel by the preposterous drift of our society, we have to remember that God is unfazed by it, He is unwilling that the lost would perish, and He is undeterred from His wonderful plan.

GOD IS UNFAZED BY THE WORLD AND ITS PATTERNS

The world is cray and getting crazier. The Bible told us this would happen. We live in a time when hedonism, skepticism, pluralism, and secularism rule. Still, God is unfazed by the chaos in our world today. He is sovereign, and He is working the details and circumstances of our planet out for a greater eternal good (Romans 8:28 and Ephesians 1:11). Instead of panicking about the downward spiral of things, we need to trust the Lord with His world and join Him in His mission to reach the lost.

> Some men attempt to excuse their own negligence by blaming the times. What have you and I to do with the times, except to serve our God in them. - Charles Spurgeon

GOD IS UNWILLING THAT THE LOST WOULD PERISH

Our God is a God who loves sinners. He does not want anyone to perish. He loves the lost and died for their sins so that anyone who believes in Him will be saved (John 3:16). He died for the sins of every sinner (1 John 2:2). He is drawing every person alive to Himself (John

12:32-33). He is unwilling that the lost would perish (2 Peter 3:9) and "wants everyone to be saved and to come to the knowledge of the truth" (1 Timothy 2:4). But what about us?

On July 9th, 2017, Jamel Dunn, a disabled man from Florida, drowned while five teenagers looked on, recording his drowning and mocking Him. The attitude of these teenagers rightly evoked anger and outrage. This story struck me particularly intensely as I wondered how my apathy about the lost was any different. Our Lord is unwilling that the lost would perish; we should be too. When we share His heart for the world, we will be compelled by His love to join Him in His wonderful plan.

GOD IS UNDETERRED IN HIS WONDERFUL PLAN

God's plan is the Great Commission (Matthew 28:18-20). He has promised to empower us for this plan (Acts 1:8). He has strategically placed us where He wants us for maximum eternal impact (Acts 17:26-27). The harvest is ripe; all that is missing is the workers (Matthew 9:36-38).

A recent survey found that 79% of Christians don't believe what they claim to believe. I actually manipulated that stat a bit. A November 2017 Barna survey found that 79% of believers don't feel compelled to preach the Gospel. But that's what is so scary. If we really believe the Gospel, we won't be willing not to share it. And if we don't see the need to share our faith, we have to wonder if we truly believe it. If we actually believe that the lost are really lost and heading for an eternity apart from Christ, we will do something about it. God is unfazed by the world and its patterns, He is unwilling that the lost would perish, and He is undeterred from His wonderful plan. We should be too.

MAKING AN IMPACT

Do you share Christ's heart when it comes to the lost? I think you do. Otherwise, you wouldn't be reading this. If you do, I believe you are up to this challenge. Instead of looking at evangelism as something to do when led or prompted, why not consider this your mission in each and every situation until God leads otherwise (Colossians 4:5)? Ask the Lord how He would have you embrace the call to a lifestyle of evangelism and then write down anything He conveys to you below.

_____

_____

_____

_____

_____

_____

DAY

SIX

Romans 1:16

For I am not ashamed of the gospel, because it is the power of God for salvation to everyone who believes, first to the Jew, and also to the Greek.

Have you ever been embarrassed, humiliated, or ashamed? It's not fun. I think most believers have been in situations where they have felt a hint of that about their faith. Opposition, intolerance, and bigotry are increasingly directed towards believers today, and many of us have reacted in fear. Sometimes the last thing we feel like doing is jumping in front of a firing squad!

It was even worse in Paul's day and age. Still, in that context, he proclaimed that he was not ashamed of the Gospel. Why? Because the Gospel is the revelation of God's glory, God's power, and God's salvation.

GOD'S GLORY

Paul was not ashamed of the Gospel because the Gospel displays the glory of God (2 Corinthians 4:4 and 1 Timothy 1:11). We see God's true nature and character, His love, mercy, power, and grace, expressed in the Gospel. The world desperately needs to see, hear, and understand the awe-inspiring reality of our God and His love for the lost. The Gospel is not something to be ashamed of; it is the power of God for the salvation of everyone who believes!

GOD'S POWER

The Gospel is the power of God! The Good News is that "God so loved the world that He gave his one and only Son, that whoever believes in Him shall not perish but have eternal life" (John 3:16). Sinners forgiven, lives transformed, death defeated; that is powerful! Paul calls it the power of God because it really is the power of God! Instead of trying to find the perfect evangelistic app, opportunity, or approach, we need to trust that the Gospel will accomplish great things if we will just share it with people. Tools are great, but the Gospel is most important. The Gospel alone is the avenue of salvation.

GOD'S SALVATION

The word Gospel comes from the Greek word εὐαγγέλιον (pronounced euaggelion), which means "Good News." Here's a brief summary of this Good News. God loves people and created us to be in close relationship with Him. Our sin separated us from the perfect God that made us, leaving us lost and hopeless, heading for an eternity apart from Him. Because of His great love for us, God came to this earth and paid the ultimate price for our sins. He died in our place and rose from the dead, conquering sin and death. Now, all who believe in Him and trust in Him alone as Savior and Lord will be forgiven and given eternal life. That is truly Good News!

> Keep to the gospel, then, more and more and more. Give people Christ, and nothing but Christ." - Charles Spurgeon

The Gospel reveals God's glory, power, and salvation. The world needs to hear this Good News. People beat around the bush about bad news, not good news. We've spent the past few decades on diluted messages, worldly gimmicks, and pretty much everything but the Gospel and it hasn't done us or the cause of Christ any good at all. It is time to pass on sheepish and tepid, socially palatable approaches and share the Good News boldly, fearlessly, and clearly as we should (Ephesians 6:19-20 and Colossians 4:3-4). It is time to get fired up about the best thing anyone ever got fired up about!

MAKING AN IMPACT

You might feel like a milquetoast believer, but in and through Him you can be as bold as a lion (Proverbs 28:1)! Take a minute to ask the Lord how fear, pride, or insecurities have kept you from sharing the Gospel boldly. Write down anything He reveals to you below. Then, ask Him to forgive you and empower you to share the Good News fearlessly. He will (Acts 1:8).

_____

_____

_____

_____

_____

— DAY —
SEVEN

Proverbs 11:30 (NIV)

The fruit of the righteous is a tree of life, and he who wins souls is wise.

Since you are going through a devotional titled *Everyday Impact*, I assume you are one of the few who is not content with apathy and passivity. I believe you want to make an impact for Christ. When Jesus called His first disciples, He told them He would make them fishers of men (Matthew 4:19). Later, He told them that He had appointed them to bear fruit that would last (John 15:16). He desires the same for us who follow Him today!

If you yearn to make a difference, this morning's devotional is for you. Today's passage reminds us of the fruit of the righteous, the fate of the lost, and the focus of the wise.

THE FRUIT OF THE RIGHTEOUS

Jesus tells us that bad trees produce bad fruit and good trees produce good fruit (Matthew 7:17-19). That seems pretty straightforward. Still, there is a truth here that is easy to miss. It can be easy to get focused on the fruit more than the tree. We can't afford to get the cart ahead of the horse here. Jesus also says, "I am the vine, you are the branches. He who abides in Me, and I in him, bears much fruit; for without Me you can do nothing" (John 15:5 NIV). If you want to be fruitful, make sure to keep your fellowship with the Lord your first priority. Out of your intimacy with Him, He will produce fruit in and through you. That fruit will become a tree of life for the lost.

THE FATE OF THE LOST

Hell isn't a very popular concept, but it is biblical. Jesus says hell is real; denying that is the same as calling Him a liar. Hell is an eternal place of punishment that was prepared for the Devil and his demons (Matthew 25:41). People you know and love will end up there too though. Those who never come to faith in Jesus, those who don't respond to the Gospel, will spend eternity there (2 Thessalonians 1:8-9). Hell isn't real because I think it is a good idea or because it is popular, it is real because God says it is. He came to this earth to seek and to save the lost because He is not willing that any would perish and He desires that everyone would come to know Him (Luke 19:10, 1 Timothy 2:4, and 2 Peter 3:9). Instead of trying to wiggle out of this biblical truth, we should follow our Lord's example of lovingly pursuing the lost. This is the only wise response.

THE FOCUS OF THE WISE

If hell is real, and it is, and if people you know and love might end up there, and some inevitably will, and if we have a real solution to this problem, and we do, the only wise response is to win souls. Remember, God has given you His Great Commission and strategically aligned the details and circumstances of your life to enable you to reach people for Him (Matthew 28:18-20, Acts 17:26-27, Ephesians 2:10, and Colossians 4:5). He has even empowered you with His Spirit to enable you to share the Good News boldly (Acts 1:8).

If you believe that there's a heaven and hell and people could be going to hell or not getting eternal life, or whatever, and you think, "well, it's not worth telling them this because it would make it socially awkward" ... How much do you have to hate somebody to not proselytize? How much do you have to hate somebody to believe that everlasting life is possible and not tell them that? - Penn Jillette (a famous atheist)

Today's reminder about the fruit of the righteous, the fate of the lost, and the focus of the wise is challenging. Take a moment to go to God in prayer about this right now.

MAKING AN IMPACT

Think of a friend from your past that you never shared with. Someone you think you'd be able to reconnect with through social media, mutual friends, or some other avenue. Write their name below. Ask God to help you find them for the point of reaching them. Then, take the initiative to contact them, and ask God to help you think of a good way to share with them.

DAY
EIGHT

Proverbs 24:10-12

If you do nothing in a difficult time, your strength is limited. Rescue those being taken off to death, and save those stumbling toward slaughter. If you say, "But we didn't know about this," won't He who weighs hearts consider it? Won't He who protects your life know? Won't He repay a person according to his work?

The Proverbs are full of wisdom about a host of different issues. This particular passage describes the wisdom of protecting those heading towards disaster. This obviously applies to the topic of evangelism! We briefly talked about the concept of hell yesterday, and we will revisit it again today. The bottom line is if we love the Lord and if we love the lost we will be preoccupied with His mission to rescue them.

There are three takeaways I hope you'll remember from this short Proverb. These are the power of God, the purpose of God, and the promise of God.

THE POWER OF GOD

This Proverb begins with a stunning statement. It says, "If you do nothing in a difficult time, your strength is limited." I think it is safe to say that we've all felt powerless and weak and have blown evangelistic opportunities in the past. If you can relate, you're not alone! Thankfully, God hasn't called us to muster up our own strength for evangelism. He has promised to empower us by His Holy Spirit for bold evangelism (Acts 1:8). God isn't looking for superheroes, He simply wants us to be willing to let Him do what only He can through us. If you are willing, He will powerfully use you for His amazing purpose.

THE PURPOSE OF GOD

God has invited each of us to partner with Him in the greatest rescue plan ever conceived. People all around us really are "stumbling toward slaughter." That is a grim reality, but there is a purpose for each of us in the midst of it. Our job is to compassionately snatch them from the fire (Jude 1:22-23). So many people around us today really are heading for an eternity in hell. The eternal lives of millions are on the line, and we have a role to play in God's plan to save them. There's a promise that comes with this as well.

THE PROMISE OF GOD

This Proverb promises us that God, who sees every action and knows every motive, will reward us for what we do. Believers can rest assured that their salvation is secure because of Christ's work at the cross and their decision to believe in Him (John 1:12 and Ephesians 2:8-9). The judgment of believers will be about reward, not punishment (1 Corinthians 3:12-15 and 2 Corinthians 5:10). Now we can live every day with our eyes set on Christ and our focus on eternity knowing it will be well worth every sacrifice we make for Him today (2 Corinthians 4:16-18 and Hebrews 12:1-2).

If they're breathing, they need Jesus."
- Mark Cahill

You were made for this challenge and you were born for this hour. Your life is not insignificant. God has molded you and prepared you over the course of your life for an extraordinary purpose. Now is the time to step out in faith, full of the power of His Holy Spirit, and available to Him for His purposes in this world. He will use you! That's a guarantee. As you step out, don't forget His power, purpose, or promise.

MAKING AN IMPACT

We haven't talked about it yet, but this passage does contain a warning as well. It says, "If you say, 'But we didn't know about this,' won't He who weighs hearts consider it?" Each of us has rationalized and made excuses for not sharing our faith in the past. This passage tells us that's not a good way to go. What excuses have you used in the past? Write them out below. Then, decide not to fall for those again in the future!

_____

_____

_____

_____

_____

DAY
NINE

Matthew 4:18-20

As He was walking along the Sea of Galilee, He saw two brothers, Simon (who is called Peter), and his brother Andrew. They were casting a net into the sea — for they were fishermen. "Follow me," He told them, "and I will make you fish for people." Immediately they left their nets and followed Him.

In the summer of 2000, my dad invited me on a fishing trip to Canada. It was a fantastic adventure. Our outfitter knew the area and provided everything we needed for a great time. The expedition included some of the best fishing we had ever seen. I also caught the catch of a lifetime on the trip, a giant tiger muskie that I still tell my kids about today! Whether you like fishing or not, I know you'll get a lot out of today's brief encouragement that focuses on the outfitter, the expedition, and the catch of a lifetime.

THE OUTFITTER

The way Jesus called these disciples was not typical. Rabbis in Jesus' time weren't interested in men like these; most would wait for more qualified candidates to apply to follow them. Jesus obliterated convention and sought these men out for a purpose. He told them, "Follow me and I will make you fish for people." And they did. These men left everything and followed Him on an expedition of soul-winning.

THE EXPEDITION

We find Jesus' call to these disciples in the other synoptic Gospels as well (see Mark 1 and Luke 5). In each case the invitation is the same, to come and become fishers of people. This is astounding. These men were already fairly comfortable, enjoying a decent living. Fishing was a good occupation back then and having boats and nets was pretty much the same as owning a small business. They left it all for Him.

It's also important to remember that fishing was different then. These men weren't using poles to catch a fish at a time. They were using nets and fishing for large quantities of fish (remember Luke 5:6-7 and John 21:11). I doubt they thought Jesus was calling them to a lifetime of catching a person here or there. They clearly understood He was calling them to lives of great impact.

Jesus challenged them to forsake their comfort zones and follow Him, promising them a life of impact and influence that would transcend anything else they would ever experience. Joining the Outfitter on this expedition turned out to be the catch of a lifetime.

THE CATCH OF A LIFETIME

Opportunities like this didn't come up very often in Galilee. Come to think of it, they don't really come up ever or anywhere. The opportunity to follow God incarnate as He walked this earth, to see Him teaching and doing miracles, and to join Him in His work. This truly was the catch of a lifetime, and it was far greater than any catch they had ever had on the Sea of Galilee. Immediately they left their nets and followed Him.

> A bad day fishing is better than a good day at work. - A familiar fishing adage.

You've probably seen today's quote on t-shirts and bumper stickers. It's obviously funny, but it actually makes a ton of sense in light of today's devotional. Even the slowest days of kingdom work are greater than the greatest days of worldly work! We've been invited to join the ultimate Outfitter on the greatest expedition, and that is definitely the catch of a lifetime.

MAKING AN IMPACT

When Jesus called these disciples, they left their possessions, occupations, and reputations in Galilee to follow Him on His mission. We have been called to the same eternally significant work (Matthew 28:18-20). What things hold you back or get in your way concerning your calling? Ask the Lord to reveal them to you and then, as He does, write them down below and surrender them to Him, making yourself available to follow Him and fish for people. You will never regret it.

DAY
TEN

Psalm 51:12-13 (NIV)

Restore to me the joy of your salvation and grant me a willing spirit, to sustain me. Then I will teach transgressors your ways, and sinners will turn back to you.

You have been called by the God of the universe to something far greater than yourself, something that will make an impact on all of eternity. If you feel like you are less than capable of this, you are correct. No one is qualified for God's Great Commission on their own. Anyone who doesn't have a sense of inadequacy when it comes to doing God's work doesn't have a clue.

David wrote this Psalm at the lowest point in his life, having just committed adultery and murder. If anyone could have pulled the "I'm not good enough to tell other people about God" card, it would have been David. He does the opposite. He goes to the Lord, confesses his sin, and then boldly proclaims His desire to help sinners find God. David was approved by God, available for God's work, and all in on God's plan.

APPROVED BY GOD

David understood that God's forgiveness was all he needed to be able to step out into the purpose God had for him. Paul did too. Paul had a past that would have made David feel good about himself. He had persecuted God's people violently and mercilessly. He could have let that stop him from all that God had for him. He didn't. He understood that he was forgiven and that God had made him competent for ministry (2 Corinthians 3:5-6). If God can use adulterers, murderers, and Christian killers, He can use you too. If you have trusted in Christ as Savior and Lord, you have been forgiven and approved for His work. Now all you need to do is to make yourself available to be used by Him.

I am the worst of all sinners. - Paul
(paraphrasing 1 Timothy 1:15-16).

28

AVAILABLE FOR GOD'S WORK

Many of us have used the "I'm not good enough to tell other people about God" excuse in the past. There are others that we often use too. Fear is a big one. The fear of rejection is enough to dissuade even the most confident Christians from evangelism. Many believers don't share their faith because they just don't know how. Whatever has kept you from sharing your faith in the past, it doesn't have to any longer.

You aren't good enough on your own, but He forgives you and approves you for His work. Evangelism can be scary, but He empowers us by His Spirit for courageous ministry. Most believers have never had great evangelism training. Still, God can and will use you if you are willing. The Holy Spirit is able to give you the words to say (we see that principle in Matthew 10:20, Mark 13:11, Luke 12:11-12, and 21:15). All you need to do is make yourself available for God's work and decide to be all in on His plan.

ALL IN ON GOD'S PLAN

Whether you feel inadequate, afraid, or unprepared, He desires to use you in great ways. The Gospel doesn't change lives because of our qualifications. The Gospel is the power of God unto salvation. You can trust that it will do its work when you simply share it. That being said, you can decide today not to let anything stop you from a life of sharing the Good News.

Keep growing in the areas that used to keep you from ministry. Choose to walk with Him in such a way that your life will point others to Him. Choose to trust Him with any fears you may have. Finally, be diligent about getting the training and tools you need. Remember, because of Him and Him alone you are approved for this work. Now, make yourself available to be used and go all in on His plan.

MAKING AN IMPACT

Have any of the three excuses listed today (I'm not good enough, I'm too scared, or I don't know how) kept you from sharing your faith? Have others? Write them down below. Then, based on today's devotional, write out why you won't let these get in your way next time.

_____

_____

_____

_____

DAY

ELEVEN

2 Corinthians 5:14-20

For the love of Christ compels us, since we have reached this conclusion: If one died for all, then all died. And He died for all so that those who live should no longer live for themselves, but for the one who died for them and was raised. From now on, then, we do not know anyone from a worldly perspective. Even if we have known Christ from a worldly perspective, yet now we no longer know Him in this way. Therefore, if anyone is in Christ, he is a new creation; the old has passed away, and see, the new has come! Everything is from God, who has reconciled us to Himself through Christ and has given us the ministry of reconciliation. That is, in Christ, God was reconciling the world to Himself, not counting their trespasses against them, and He has committed the message of reconciliation to us. Therefore, we are ambassadors for Christ, since God is making His appeal through us. We plead on Christ's behalf: "Be reconciled to God."

In the spring of 1999, John Fildes, a freshman college student who had been a member of the Bahai faith, put his trust in Christ. He was never the same again. A short time later, he spent Valentine's Day walking around campus wearing a sandwich board cutout of a heart that said, "Jesus is my Valentine," telling people God loved them! His life became consumed with sacrificial service for the Lord. His perspective of others changed as He began to see everyone with an eternal perspective. That caused him to share his faith boldly; in his dorm, in his classes, and across the campus. Inside out transformation might look different for different people but it should be the norm in the Christian life!

When Christ comes into a life, He radically remakes it. When we surrender to Him as Savior and Lord, He fundamentally renews us. That change motivates us to sacrifice willingly, see differently, and serve faithfully.

SACRIFICING WILLINGLY

In this challenging passage, Paul tells us that the love of Christ, evidenced by His sacrifice for us, compels us to live for Him rather than ourselves. Sacrificially living for the Lord is true worship (Romans 12:1). It is less of a sacrificial duty and more of a natural response to His love. Christ's love compels us to love and serve Him, and it changes our entire outlook on life.

If a commission by an earthly king is considered an honor, how can a commission by a Heavenly King be considered a sacrifice? - David Livingstone

---

SEEING DIFFERENTLY

When the Gospel gets a hold of someone, it changes the way they view God, themselves, and those around them. Now, we see everything through the lens of the Gospel. We see our Savior as our Lord, we see ourselves as new creations in Him, and we see the lost as people who God loves and who He desires to reach. That perspective change motivates faithful service.

SERVING FAITHFULLY

You are Christ's ambassador! It is an honor and a privilege to represent the Lord in this world. Ambassadors exist to communicate the words and desires of their leaders to the people they are sent to. Whatever occupations or obligations you may have, God has placed you in those areas to be His ambassador. This is your ultimate mission. We have been called to faithfully serve as His ambassadors, sharing His message of love and reconciliation with the lost wherever we go and whatever we do.

God has committed the message of reconciliation to us and called us to be His ambassadors. It is a joy and a privilege to serve Him. Christ's love compels us to sacrifice willingly, to see differently, and to serve faithfully.

MAKING AN IMPACT

Ask God to show you a specific way He would have you serve as His ambassador in your school, workplace, or neighborhood this week. Write down anything He puts on your mind.

DAY
TWELVE

Acts 20:24 (NIV)

However, I consider my life worth nothing to me, if only I may finish the race and complete the task the Lord Jesus has given me - the task of testifying to the gospel of God's grace.

Eric Liddell was a prestigious, gold medal-winning British runner who didn't let success or fame distract him from his ultimate calling. He refused to run on Sundays, choosing instead to keep that day devoted to the Lord. He also left his life as a famous athlete at the height of his career to become a missionary to China, where he ended up spending the rest of his life. Eric knew which race mattered most and he devoted his life on this earth to the only task that would have an eternal impact.

Paul did too. He left a life of position and prominence for one of purpose and persecution. He was convinced that knowing and serving Jesus was far greater than anything else in life (Philippians 3:7-8). His life and example, which are articulated so clearly in today's passage, are an encouragement for each of us today. Like Paul, we all have one life to live, one race to run, and one call to complete.

ONE LIFE TO LIVE

Paul considered his life worth nothing outside of knowing and serving the Lord and accomplishing the purpose God had for him. He knew that he only had one life to live and he wasn't about to let the things of this world sidetrack him from knowing, loving, and serving the Lord. He willingly gave up everything for the Lord, and he ran his race with commitment and diligence.

ONE RACE TO RUN

Paul was unwilling to be hindered in his race (Galatians 2:2 and Philippians 2:16). He ran his race, preaching the Gospel, with discipline, commitment, and an eternal perspective (1 Corinthians 9:24-27). Paul was unwaveringly focused on his calling and purpose, the task God had given him; we should be too.

ONE CALL TO COMPLETE

Paul's calling, in his own words, was "the task of testifying to the gospel of God's grace." Preaching the Good News was his custom, his habit, and his life commitment (Acts 17:2). It should be ours also.

We have been called to shine brightly (Matthew 5:15-16), to make the most of every opportunity (Colossians 4:5), and to witness boldly (Acts 1:8). We have been invited to co-labor with the Lord in His redemptive work (1 Corinthians 3:9). We have been given the Great Commission (Matthew 28:18-20). The task of testifying to the Gospel of God's grace was not just Paul's calling; it is ours as well.

Only one life, 'twill soon be past, Only what's done for Christ will last. - C. T. Studd (another famous British athlete, a cricket player, who left everything to serve on the mission field.)

You only have one life to live on this planet. Live it with an eternal perspective (2 Corinthians 4:18). You have been given one race to run; run it with your eyes set on Jesus (Hebrews 12:1-2). You have been given a call to complete; do that with diligence, testifying to the Gospel of God's grace in each and every situation you can.

MAKING AN IMPACT

The details and responsibilities of life can easily distract us from the mission that God has for us. Paul's laser beam focus on preaching the Gospel is rarely seen among believers today. It doesn't have to be that way. Partnering with the Lord in eternally significant work is exciting, and it is a fundamental aspect of the abundant life Jesus promises (John 10:10). Ask the Lord how He would have you elevate evangelism to a priority in your life. Write down whatever He prompts below. Then, pray and ask the Lord to rekindle in you a heart for reaching the lost.

— DAY —
THIRTEEN

Psalm 96:2 (NIV)

Sing to the LORD; bless His name. Each day proclaim the good news that He saves.

A Harvard study, which was published in 2018, revealed the shocking findings that a nutritious diet, healthy body weight, frequent exercise, and avoidance of smoking and excessive drinking dramatically improved people's health. The research even demonstrated that these habits could increase life expectancy by more than a decade. Okay, maybe those findings aren't that surprising. The main point is important though: the healthy choices we make and the little things we do each day really matter!

Just like there are habits that are vital to overall physical health, there are practices that are essential for our spiritual growth as well. Spending time in God's Word on a daily basis is vitally important (Psalm 1:1-3 and Matthew 4:4). Praying and talking with the Lord throughout each and every day is too (Psalm 88:9 and 1 Thessalonians 5:17). Praising God and acknowledging Him as Lord in our lives is an absolutely fundamental practice (Psalm 145:2). So is fellowshipping with other believers (Acts 2:46, Hebrews 3:13, and 10:24-25). Today's passage also lists evangelism as an important daily practice!

Psalm 96:2 tells us to proclaim the Good News that He saves each day. Did you catch that? The Bible tells us to share our faith each and every day! God's commands are not burdensome (1 John 5:3). Obeying them is good for us! Here are seven benefits of sharing your faith daily.

YOU WILL ENCOUNTER NEW FRIENDS
You don't have to be friends with someone before you can witness to them. Sharing your faith is a great way to meet new people. People you reach will become close friends (Acts 2:47).

YOU WILL EMBOLDEN FELLOW BELIEVERS
Your example will impact other believers positively, and that will lead to stronger relationships with them (1 Timothy 4:12).

YOU WILL EXPERIENCE GREAT ADVENTURES

Instead of looking at each day with a sense of monotony, you'll find meaning in every opportunity, and that is exciting (Colossians 4:5).

YOU WILL EFFECT LASTING CHANGE

Your life will be one of impact and influence and, through the Holy Spirit's enabling, you will be making a difference that lasts through eternity (1 Corinthians 15:58).

YOU WILL ELUCIDATE A SENSE OF IDENTITY

You will be constantly reminded of who God is, who you are in Him, and what He has done for you (2 Corinthians 5:17).

YOU WILL ELIMINATE MEANINGLESSNESS

You will begin to have a sense of purpose and significance that will come to define each and every day (Ephesians 2:8-10).

YOU WILL ENJOY DEEP FELLOWSHIP WITH CHRIST

This is the best benefit. As you tell others about Jesus, you'll find yourself growing closer to Him (John 15:5 and 1 Corinthians 3:9). Our fellowship with the Lord will motivate obedience in evangelism and evangelism will grow our closeness with Him too. It's an amazing cycle!

There are no unhappy obedient Christians, and there are no happy disobedient Christians. - Bill Bright

---

2 Corinthians 6:2 tells us that today is the day of salvation. Why not proclaim that each day? Every day is a good day to tell others the Good News that He saves! Serving the Lord and sharing the Good News that He saves is also an important part of the abundant life Jesus promises (John 10:10 and Romans 12:11).

MAKING AN IMPACT

Since so few believers share their faith, we might be tempted to feel good about ourselves if we witness at all, even if only infrequently. Ask the Lord to show you any areas you have been complacent. Write them down below. Ask Him to forgive you and to embolden you in those areas.

_____

_____

_____

_____

DAY
FOURTEEN

Romans 10:13-15

For everyone who calls on the name of the Lord will be saved. How, then, can they call on Him they have not believed in? And how can they believe without hearing about Him? And how can they hear without a preacher? And how can they preach unless they are sent? As it is written: How beautiful are the feet of those who bring good news.

In the fall of 2018, John Chau is presumed to have been killed while attempting to bring the Gospel to the North Sentinelese, one of the most isolated tribes on the planet. Shortly before his mission, he wrote a note to his family. He expressed his desire not to die and affirmed his willingness to trust God with his life. He wrote, "You guys might think I'm crazy in all this but I think it's worthwhile to declare Jesus to these people." He was right!

The lost must be reached, and the Gospel must be preached. If we really believe what we say we believe, we can't stay silent about it. We must guard against any lies that would convince us otherwise. We have the world's most important message and have been given the mandate of being messengers who will spread it.

THE MESSAGE

The message is clear. Anyone who believes in Jesus as Savior and Lord will be saved (John 3:16, Acts 16:31, and Ephesians 2:8-9). God loves people and created us for a relationship with Himself. Unfortunately, our sin and rebellion have separated us from Him. He came to this earth and died on the cross for our sins. Now all who believe in Him and receive His free gift of salvation will be saved. This message must be preached to people everywhere (Mark 13:10). That is the mandate from our Savior.

THE MANDATE

Jesus has given us the mandate to "Go and make disciples of all nations" (Matthew 28:19). We have been sent. The only question we need to worry about now is whether or not we will go as His messengers.

THE MESSENGERS

You and I are the messengers. The harvest is ripe, but the workers are few (Matthew 9:37). We must preach the Gospel. We cannot stay silent.

Preach the Gospel, and since it's necessary, use words.
- Ed Stetzer

Satan is constantly tempting us to minimize the message, ignore the mandate of our Savior, and abdicate the responsibility of being His messengers. We can't let our enemy's lies keep us from our Lord's call.

MAKING AN IMPACT

One lie you'll often hear is a misquote of Saint Francis of Assisi that says, "Preach always, use words if necessary." Today's passage obliterates that lie. Here are some other lies we've all heard.

It is a lie that most people aren't interested; the truth is that the harvest is ripe (Matthew 9:37). It is a lie that you must have the gift of evangelism; the truth is that we're all called and empowered (Acts 1:8). It is a lie that you have to be trendy and relevant first; the truth is that God uses even the weak (1 Corinthians 1:27). It is a lie that you must earn the right to be heard; the truth is that Jesus already did that (John 3:16). It is a lie that only the destitute need Jesus; the truth is that God wants everyone to be saved (1 Timothy 2:4). It is a lie that older people aren't interested; the truth is that God is working on every heart (John 12:32-33). It is a lie that resources and tracts won't work; the truth is that the Gospel, in any format, is powerful (Romans 1:16). It is a lie that all is lost if someone gets offended; the truth is that some people will get offended (Matthew 10:22). It is a lie that you need to wait until you find a perfect method; the truth is that sowing seed is the greatest need (Matthew 13:1-9).

What lies have you believed about evangelism? Write them below, along with the truth that contradicts them.

— DAY —
FIFTEEN

Matthew 12:34 B (NKJV)

...out of the abundance of the heart the mouth speaks.

I have a very special friend. Her name is Joan Ross. One thing I love about Joan is her passion for Jesus and telling others about Him. We've had many evangelistic adventures together. Joan didn't come to know Jesus until she was fifty-nine. Now, years later, she is still overcome with the joy of what God has done in her life, and she wants everyone to know about Him.

When someone is truly transformed by Jesus, they can't help but treasure Him (Luke 7:47 and 1 John 4:19). When we treasure our Savior, we can't help but speak about Him. If we find ourselves struggling to tell others about Jesus, we need to do a little introspection to see what the real issue is. We each have a survey to take, a Savior to treasure, and a story to tell.

A SURVEY TO TAKE

What do you talk about? Before going any further, write out the top things you talk about below:

1. _____.

2. _____.

3. _____.

4. _____.

Jesus tells us that the mouth speaks about what the heart is full of. James 3:9-12 reiterates the same principle. If we fail to treasure Christ, no amount of evangelism training will fix the issue. Taking a survey of what we talk about is a good way to diagnose what we really treasure. If that reveals a deficiency in evangelism, drawing near to Jesus and treasuring Him is the perfect antidote.

A SAVIOR TO TREASURE

A treasure always transforms the one who finds it (Matthew 13:44-46). When we see and value Jesus for who He really is and what He has really done for us, everything changes. At the end of the day, there are only two ways to view our Savior: as a treasure or a trinket. If He is our treasure, our life and speech will revolve around Him and His work. As we draw near and grow close to Him, He will assume His rightful place in our hearts, and we will be unable to stop telling of Him!

A STORY TO TELL

King David put it this way, "Because your love is better than life, my lips will glorify you" (Psalm 63:3 NIV). When a person becomes consumed with love for their Savior, they will inevitably tell others the story of what He has done in their lives. We have a story to tell, a story of a God that loves people and died and rose again to give them eternal life. That story needs to be told, and believers who treasure their Savior won't be able to help but tell it.

The question of speaking to souls is a question of personal love to the Lord Jesus Christ. Do not say you have no gift for it. Do you love Christ? If so, you will never lose an opportunity of speaking a word for Him. - G.V. Wigram

---

Evangelism is a great diagnostic of spiritual health and maturity. Our speech tells us a lot about what we value and cherish. If we treasure our Savior, we will tell others about Him and all He has done for us.

MAKING AN IMPACT

What do you talk most about? What did you write down a few minutes ago? If Christ isn't coming up in your conversations, don't panic! Focus on drawing near to Him, allowing Him to become your greatest treasure. As you do that, He will begin producing His fruit in and through you (John 15:5). The key to evangelism isn't just trying harder; the key is drawing near to Jesus so He will exude naturally in each conversation you find yourself in. Write out one key way you will begin drawing closer to Jesus each day below.

_____

_____

_____

_____

DAY

SIXTEEN

1 Corinthians 9:16-17

For preaching the Good News is not something I can boast about. I am compelled by God to do it. How terrible for me if I didn't do it! If I were doing this of my own free will, then I would deserve payment. But God has chosen me and given me this sacred trust, and I have no choice.

I'm going to tell you a very embarrassing story. Once, as a young father, I took my six-month-old daughter on a few errands in town. I ended up getting sidetracked by my to-do list, and I completely forgot she was in the car with me. About three stops and an hour later I returned home. As I walked into my house, I realized my daughter wasn't with me. Instantly, I was overcome with a terrifying sense of fear and panic. I ran out to my car and found her sleeping happily. It was a cool spring day, and everything turned out fine. I learned a lesson that day: never take a responsibility flippantly! For the next few years, every time I drove with my kids in the car, I would take my left shoe off and put it in the back by their car seats so I couldn't repeat that mistake!

In this passage, Paul calls preaching the Gospel a sacred trust! If ever there was a responsibility not to take lightly, this is it! We, like Paul, have a task to accomplish, a truth to acknowledge, and a trust to accept.

A TASK TO ACCOMPLISH

Paul was compelled by God, and by his love for the Lord and the lost, to preach the Gospel (2 Corinthians 5:14). His call to this work had been convincing and clear (Acts 9:1-31). Still, like any of us, he had a choice to make. To do the work or not to. He chose to persevere, even in the face of overwhelming obstacles and outrageous opposition (2 Corinthians 11:23-29). This call wasn't just for Paul; we have been charged with reaching the lost for Christ as well; God's Word makes our invitation to this work clear (Matthew 5:15-16, 28:18-20, and Acts 1:8). Like Paul, we have a task to accomplish. That is a truth we need to acknowledge.

> The One who calls you to go into all the world and preach
> the Gospel to every creature is the One who by your
> consent, goes into all the world and preaches the Gospel
> to every creature through you! - Major Ian Thomas

A TRUTH TO ACKNOWLEDGE

Paul understood who he was in Christ, what he was here for, and why the work he had been called to was so important. His response to that truth was adamant, "How terrible for me if I didn't do it!" Some translations translate that, "woe to me if I do not preach the gospel." Paul was convinced there was no better way to invest his life (Acts 20:24). If God is who He says He is, and if we are who He says we are, and if the lost need Him like He says they do, how else could we respond? This isn't just a deductive response, we've also been given a trust from our Lord.

A TRUST TO ACCEPT

Paul calls preaching the Gospel a "trust" here. Some translations translate it as "sacred trust." He said he had no choice but to respond. The same is true of us. Jesus Christ, God incarnate, Creator and Sustainer of the universe, the Savior of the world has called you and me to take His message throughout the world. The only sensible response is yes; a yes with conviction, passion, and application. We have been given a sacred trust, and we must be faithful (1 Corinthians 4:2).

God wants everyone to be saved and none to perish (1 Timothy 2:4 and 2 Peter 3:9). There is a task to accomplish, a truth to acknowledge, and a trust to accept. We must be faithful (Matthew 15:14-30).

MAKING AN IMPACT

Spend a moment processing today's devotional in prayer. Ask God to show you how He would have you steward the call to evangelism. Remember my left shoe solution; that simple idea helped me faithfully steward the trust of my child. Can you think of a left shoe type of solution for evangelism, something that would keep you from missing opportunities? Write it down below.

_____

_____

_____

_____

SEVENTEEN

Matthew 5:15-16

No one lights a lamp and puts it under a basket, but rather on a lamp stand, and it gives light for all who are in the house. In the same way, let your light shine before others, so that they may see your good works and give glory to your Father in heaven.

Have you ever been lost in the dark? It's not fun. It's scary. It can be dangerous. It feels hopeless. A light, even the smallest candle, changes everything! The world is getting darker. That shouldn't surprise us; God promised us it would (Matthew 24:4-8 and 2 Timothy 3:1-5). We aren't told to be lights or to shine the light; we are told that we are lights in this dark world! The light can't help but shine.

The world is getting darker. Jesus is the light of the world (John 8:12). Every believer has been called to reflect the light, raise the light, and radiate the light in the midst of the darkness.

REFLECTING THE LIGHT

The moon has no light of its own; it simply reflects the light of the sun. Because of its position in relation to the sun, it can't stop from reflecting the sun's light. The same is true for those who love and follow Jesus. When we put our faith in Him as Savior and Lord, He illuminates our lives and shines His light through us (John 12:46). We have no light in and of ourselves but, because of our relationship with Him and who we are in Him, His light is reflected in and through our lives, unless we cover it up! Jesus makes it clear that we shouldn't cover up our light but should raise it high for all to see!

RAISING THE LIGHT

If you have trusted in Him as Savior and Lord, you have the Ultimate Light living in you. Jesus says the only two options are to put it under a basket or on a lamp stand. Many Christians do the former, trying to blend in and not offend, thinking they might influence the lost if they can be indistinguishable from them. Jesus tells us to let our light shine, not to cover it, but to raise it high. In every relationship, conversation, and circumstance, we have a choice to obscure the light or elevate it. The world desperately needs Jesus. Now more than ever, we need to raise Him high and radiate His light wherever we go.

> Could a mariner sit idle if he heard the drowning cry?
> Could a doctor sit in comfort and just let his patients
> die? Could a fireman sit idle, let men burn and give
> no hand? Can you sit at ease in Zion with the world
> around you damned? - Leonard Ravenhill

RADIATING THE LIGHT

Jesus says we are to let our light shine so people will see our good works and find Him. Good works can't be separated from the message of the Gospel. Telling others about Jesus is also a good work in and of itself! Paul calls preaching the Good News "the work of the Gospel" (Philippians 2:22 and 4:3). The insidious "preach always, use words if necessary" lie has plagued Christendom for too long; good works are not the full extent of the Gospel work we need to be preoccupied with. Good works are vitally important, but Christ's message can't be spread silently (Romans 10:13-15). The Good News of His salvation is the light the world needs (2 Corinthians 4:4). We can't pick between the two; we need both to demonstrate the Gospel with our works and to communicate it with our words.

We have been given a sacred trust of reflecting the light, raising the light, and radiating the light in an increasingly dark world. As you walk with Christ and yield to Him, He will shine through you, beaming into the darkness everywhere you go.

MAKING AN IMPACT

Sharing our faith is a lot less complicated than we often make it. We need to focus less on how to shine the light and more on growing closer to Jesus and letting Him shine through us. Ask Him to reveal any areas that you have been covering up His light. Write down anything He shows you. Then, confess that to Him and ask Him to empower you to elevate the light, with both your actions and your words, in those areas.

43

DAY
EIGHTEEN

Acts 1:8

But you will receive power when the Holy Spirit has come on you, and you will be my witnesses in Jerusalem, in all Judea and Samaria, and to the end of the earth.

I'm sure you've wrestled with insecurity and inadequacy concerning evangelism. I have, and to be honest, after decades of sharing my faith, I still do. D.L. Moody understood something that we need to grasp as well; he wrote, "There is not a better evangelist in the world than the Holy Spirit." In today's verse, Jesus promises us that His Holy Spirit will empower us for evangelism.

This truth will revolutionize your life. If you are willing, He will empower you to do what only He can, as you make yourself available for His work. You are not alone; you have been endowed with God's power, entrusted with God's purpose, and equipped with God's plan.

WE HAVE BEEN ENDOWED WITH GOD'S POWER

If you have believed in Jesus as Savior and Lord, the Bible says you have been given the Holy Spirit and His power is available for you (John 7:37-39, 1 Corinthians 3:16, 6:19, 12:13, and Ephesians 1:13). God's Word commands us to be continually filled with His Spirit (Ephesians 5:18). J. Oswald Sanders explains, "To be filled with the Spirit means simply that the Christian voluntarily surrenders life and will to the Spirit. Through faith, the believer's personality is permeated, mastered, and controlled by the Spirit." As you consciously yield to Him and allow Him to fill and control you, you will experience His power in evangelism. I will give you an easy to remember acronym for being filled with His power in just a minute. But first, remember the reason for that power: God's purpose!

Success in witnessing is simply taking the initiative to share Christ in the power of the Holy Spirit and leaving the results to God. The only way we ever fail in our witness is if we fail to witness. - Bill Bright

WE HAVE BEEN ENTRUSTED WITH GOD'S PURPOSE

Jesus correlates the power of the Holy Spirit with witnessing for Him. God doesn't empower us for our purposes; He empowers us for His purposes! He desires to empower us for His purpose of seeking and saving the lost (Luke 19:10). He has given us an incredible plan for doing that.

WE HAVE BEEN EQUIPPED WITH GOD'S PLAN.

God's plan has always been to reach every nation (Genesis 22:18 and Psalm 82:8). That will come to pass (Revelation 5:9 and 7:9). His strategy involves evangelism and discipleship that begin where you are at, your Jerusalem so to say, and multiply out from there to all the earth (Matthew 28:18-20, Acts 17:26-27, and 2 Timothy 2:2).

You and I have the incredible privilege of walking in the Lord's power as we join Him in His purpose and plan!

MAKING AN IMPACT

The POWER acronym is a simple way to remember how to experience His filling and power.

Present yourself to God, surrendering to Him to be used in evangelism (Romans 12:1-2).

Own up to any sin He makes you aware of in this area and confess it to Him; He will forgive you (1 John 1:9).

Want to honor God as His witness, choosing to live a Spirit-filled and empowered life (Matthew 5:6).

Experience His power for evangelism, asking Him to fill you with His Spirit and believing He will (James 1:6-7 and 1 John 5:14-15).

Rely on Him, taking a step of faith to share your faith and trusting He will empower you for that (2 Corinthians 5:7).

Ask God to show you a situation you could apply this in. Write it down below and then take a step of faith into that. You don't have what it takes, but the Holy Spirit in you does!

NINETEEN

Colossians 4:2-6 (NIV)

Devote yourselves to prayer, being watchful and thankful. And pray for us, too, that God may open a door for our message, so that we may proclaim the mystery of Christ, for which I am in chains. Pray that I may proclaim it clearly, as I should. Be wise in the way you act toward outsiders; make the most of every opportunity. Let your conversation be always full of grace, seasoned with salt, so that you may know how to answer everyone.

Austin Krokos has been a close friend and accountability partner. When one of his children had a terrifying medical emergency, he told me, "God has given me lots of peace. Praying for lost doctors that have the worst disease." Even when his child's life was on the line, he was making the most of the opportunity to reach the lost in the hospital, praying for them and sharing with them.

Today's passage commands us to "make the most of every opportunity." It also gives us four clear ways to do that. These include praying fervently, sharing clearly, acting strategically, and speaking intentionally.

PRAYING FERVENTLY

In the context of evangelism, Paul tells us to be devoted to prayer. This involves praying for evangelism and evangelists and for the lost as well (1 Timothy 2:1-3). We have the privilege of joining God in praying for evangelistic work and workers (Matthew 9:38) and for the lost that need our Savior. Praying is important, but it doesn't end there; we're also called to share!

SHARING CLEARLY

Paul tells us the Gospel must be preached clearly. The word "clearly" comes from the Greek word **φανερόω** (pronounced phaneroó), which means to make known, understood, clear, visible, and manifest.

We must present the Gospel clearly, carefully articulating God's love, humanity's sin, Jesus' payment, and our decision. We need to keep the Gospel simple and understandable, being strategic with every opportunity!

ACTING STRATEGICALLY

We have countless opportunities each day but often miss them while waiting for a mystical prompting. If God leads you to share with someone, don't hesitate. Also, know that you don't have to wait for some celestial cue; simply acknowledge the charge of God's Word and be strategic about making the most of every opportunity. You can trust He has divinely set it all up (Acts 17:26-27 and Ephesians 2:10). Then, determine to act and speak intentionally in every circumstance!

God can use you to help win the lost. - Warren Wiersbe

SPEAKING INTENTIONALLY

Scripture is clear that we must preach the Good News with our words (Romans 10:13-15). We're told here that all of our speech should be full of grace and seasoned with salt. Every conversation with an unbeliever is an opportunity for evangelism.

We are called to make the most of every opportunity. We should do that by praying fervently, sharing clearly, acting strategically, and speaking intentionally.

MAKING AN IMPACT

An old saying says, "first talk to God about people and then talk to people about God." That's true, and that's the first point in today's passage. Ask God to show you five non-Christians to pray for every day. Then, write their names below and begin praying for them daily and looking for opportunities to share with them.

1. _____.

2. _____.

3. _____.

4. _____.

5. _____.

DAY
TWENTY

John 4:39

Now many Samaritans from that town believed in Him because of what the woman said when she testified, "He told me everything I ever did."

Testimonies are powerful. Just think of all the commercials you see. Personal testimonies about all sorts of products drive our economy! God used the Samaritan woman's testimony powerfully, and He wants to use yours as well. Take a minute to read the context for today's verse, John 4:1-42, and consider seven principles we find in it.

BELIEVE GOD WILL USE YOU
Jesus did and we should too.

BE EMPOWERED AND INTENTIONAL
Jesus went straight to this woman and boldly reached out to her.

BEGIN A CONVERSATION
In spite of numerous cultural taboos, Jesus began a conversation with this woman.

BEFRIEND SINNERS
Jesus was kind and respectful. We must be as well. We don't need to wait until we are friends to share but should befriend those we share with.

BUILD UP TO THE GOSPEL
Jesus intentionally directed the conversation back to the Good News He offered.

BRIEFLY SHARE YOUR TESTIMONY
That is what the Samaritan woman did, and God used her mightily.

BRING THE CONVERSATION TO THE POINT OF DECISION
Jesus did this strategically (see John 4:26) and we should too.

> ## Go for souls. Go straight for souls, and go for the worst. - William Booth

MAKING AN IMPACT

The world needs to hear our testimonies. This abbreviated version of Oasis World Ministries' One Minute Witness will help you share yours.

PART A: What three words describe your life before Christ? If you trusted Christ at a young age, describe three aspects of your sinful nature apart from Christ.

There was a time in my life when _____, _____, and _____ defined who I was.

PART B: How did you come to faith in Christ? Include the details of how you put your faith in Christ and briefly describe the key aspects of the Gospel here (God's love, your sin, Jesus' provision, and your decision to trust Him).

And then one day, (how did you hear / understand the Gospel)...

When I realized what Jesus had done for me, I (how did you respond to the Gospel)...

PART C: What three words describe your life after Christ?

Since I've met Jesus, He has changed me and now I am _____, _____, and _____.

Part D: Summarize your story with a sentence and then ask the person you're talking with if they'd like to know how Jesus could do something like this in their life.

Personalize, develop and refine this. Keep it simple and Christ-focused (1 Corinthians 2:1–2). Try keeping it to a minute. Practice it and be ready to share it often! You can also initiate a conversation by asking someone if you can ask them a question. If they say, "yes," ask, "What is the greatest thing that has ever happened to you?" Listen to them, show them you care, and then ask if you can share the greatest thing that has ever happened to you. If they say yes, share your testimony. God will use you!

DAY
TWENTY ONE

1 Corinthians 9:19–23

Although I am free from all and not anyone's slave, I have made myself a slave to everyone, in order to win more people. To the Jews I became like a Jew, to win Jews; to those under the law, like one under the law — though I myself am not under the law — to win those under the law. To those who are without the law, like one without the law — though I am not without God's law but under the law of Christ — to win those without the law. To the weak I became weak, in order to win the weak. I have become all things to all people, so that I may by every possible means save some. Now I do all this because of the Gospel, so that I may share in the blessings.

Hudson Taylor left England to serve as a missionary to China in the middle of the nineteenth century. At that time, Christian workers weren't effectively impacting that nation. Taylor changed that. One of his key approaches was to meet the Chinese where they were at by becoming like them. He left the comforts of England to become Chinese in his approach to the Chinese in order to reach the Chinese. During his time of ministry in that country, the situation changed as more and more missionaries began following Taylor there, and China began being reached. Now, more than a century later, China has one of the largest populations of believers in the world.

Paul was committed to doing whatever it took to reach anyone and everyone he possibly could with the Gospel. We should follow his example, committing to becoming all things, using all means, and reaching all people.

BECOMING ALL THINGS

Jesus is our greatest example of this. Remember how He befriended and spent time with adulterers, tax-collectors, and sinners for the point of reaching them (Matthew 9:10, 11:19, Mark 2:15-16, Luke 5:30, 7:31-39, 15:1, and 19:1-10). Sinners won't be saved when they are shunned by believers. We must follow Christ's example of meeting the lost where they are at. That might mean learning new hobbies, joining new groups, or just being faithful to reach those already around us. We can't be passive, and we can't let our comfort zones stop us. We need to become all things to all people, and we must use all means to do that.

USING ALL MEANS

What are you willing to do to reach the lost? Using all means will involve sacrificially using your time, abilities, and possessions for outreach (Romans 12:1-2). Are you willing to make that kind of sacrifice? If so, you will begin reaching all sorts of new people.

If I thought I could win one more soul to the Lord by walking on my head and playing the tambourine with my toes, I'd learn how! - William Booth

---

REACHING ALL PEOPLE

There is a world full of people who will probably never set foot inside our churches. We cannot wait for them to come to us. We have a command to go to them (Matthew 28:18-20 and Acts 1:8). We must take it seriously and determine to be intentional about doing whatever it takes, in the love and power of our Lord, to reach them any way possible, wherever they are at.

We need to be all in on becoming all things and using all means to reach all people!

MAKING AN IMPACT

Don't let your comfort zones sabotage your capacity for influence! Ask the Lord to show you someone in your sphere of influence that you have neglected sharing with for whatever reason. Ask Him to give you a plan to meet them where they are at. Write their name and the plan to reach them below. Then, begin praying for this person and this opportunity.

The person you want to reach:

How you plan to reach out:

DAY
TWENTY TWO

Ephesians 6:19-20 (NIV)

Pray also for me, that whenever I open my mouth, words may be given me so that I will fearlessly make known the mystery of the gospel, for which I am an ambassador in chains. Pray that I may declare it fearlessly, as I should.

Some of the most significant and satisfying things I have ever been a part of involved an element of risk and a little bit of fear. Snowboarding competitively, beginning a relationship with Erin, who I later married, starting a Ph.D., and launching ministries are all steps I felt inadequate for. In spite of some initial anxiety, these all became life-changing adventures. Capitulating to fear would have kept me from the abundant life Jesus promises (John 10:10).

Most of us struggle with an aspect of fear concerning evangelism. I still do, even after decades of sharing my faith. We can either give in to that fear, rationalizing our disobedience, or we can trust the Lord, stepping into the life of impact and abundance He has for us. Unfortunately, most Christians go the first route. Paul didn't. He relied on the fellowship of believers and the filling of the Spirit in His fearless proclamation of the Gospel.

THE FELLOWSHIP OF BELIEVERS

Paul asked the Ephesians to pray for Him. He could have come up with a million excuses for not sharing his faith. He could have said, "I can't share because I'm in prison," or, "I don't want to get killed," or any assortment of rationalizations. Instead, he agreed with the truth of God's Word, called a spade a spade, and sought encouragement and accountability for bold evangelism. We too should surround ourselves with Christians who will challenge us to trust God and walk in His will and strength, allowing His Spirit to empower us.

THE FILLING OF THE SPIRIT

Jesus had promised the disciples that when persecuted for His sake the Holy Spirit would empower them to speak fearlessly (Matthew 10:20,

Mark 13:11, Luke 12:11-12, and 21:15). No doubt Paul was aware of this when he asked the Ephesians to pray for this very thing. Paul relied on the Holy Spirit for the words to say and the power to say them. Instead of yielding to fear, we should follow Paul's example and the command to be filled with the Holy Spirit, and trust God to empower us for fearless evangelism (Acts 1:8 and Ephesians 5:18).

THE FEARLESSNESS OF GOD

Paul said, "Pray that I may declare it fearlessly, as I should." The Gospel should be proclaimed fearlessly. We shouldn't justify evangelistic negligence or apologize for our message. We should walk in the freedom and power of God, experiencing His fearlessness in life and ministry (Proverbs 28:1). Get in His Word and allow the truth to free you from fear (Joshua 1:8-9 and John 8:32). Share your anxieties with the Lord and allow Him to replace them with His peace (Philippians 4:6-7). Then, step into all He has for you with His power!

A nation will not be moved by timid methods.
- Luis Palau

Fear of rejection is usually one of the biggest fears most of us face. God's Word tells us we will be hated and persecuted because of Him (Matthew 10:22, John 15:18, 17:14, and 2 Timothy 1:8-9). Any opposition we face is an opportunity for evangelism (Luke 21:12-15). Jesus also promised us blessing and reward in the midst of rejection, persecution, and insults (Matthew 5:10-12). Take a few minutes to visit icommittopray.com and pray for some of the prayer requests for persecuted brothers and sisters around the world. Their examples will encourage you.

We need to embrace the possibility of rejection and not let it stop us. We can rely on the fellowship of believers and the filling of the Spirit as we fearlessly preach the Gospel.

MAKING AN IMPACT

Paul relied on the Ephesians for encouragement in evangelism. You will also benefit tremendously from fellowship and accountability with outreach focused friends. List a few of the most evangelistic friends you have below. Make it a point to spend more time with these people.

DAY
TWENTY THREE

Matthew 13:3-9

Then He told them many things in parables, saying: "Consider the sower who went out to sow. As he sowed, some seed fell along the path, and the birds came and devoured them. Other seed fell on rocky ground where it didn't have much soil, and it grew up quickly since the soil wasn't deep. But when the sun came up, it was scorched, and since it had no root, it withered away. Other seed fell among thorns, and the thorns came up and choked it. Still other seed fell on good ground and produced fruit: some a hundred, some sixty, and some thirty times what was sown. Let anyone who has ears listen."

A good friend of mine, Kirk Walker, leads a ministry on a local university campus. He and his team typically share the Gospel with around six thousand students each year. His example constantly pushes me to sow more seed. That's exactly what Jesus talks about in today's passage.

I once heard a speaker teaching on this passage. He asked, "What do you think of the sower?" After a few minutes of going back and forth with the audience, he blurted out, "He was an idiot." Everybody laughed. Then he asked, "Who sows seed on roads, on rocks, and in weeds?" He concluded, "God hasn't called us to be soil specialists, He has called us to be seed chuckers!"

There are no perfect programs or ministry magic bullets. We have to remember that the Gospel, pure and simple, is the power of God for salvation (Romans 1:16). We need to join the Lord in His Great Commission work, participating purposefully, planting plentifully, and persevering patiently.

PARTICIPATING PURPOSEFULLY

We have been given a sacred trust (1 Corinthians 9:17). We have been invited to be co-laborers with the Lord Himself (1 Corinthians 3:9). We have been given the Great Commission and promised the power of

His Holy Spirit for its fulfillment (Matthew 28:18-20 and Acts 1:8). How can we abdicate this privilege or shirk this responsibility? What is more important than the eternal destination of millions of souls? The harvest is plentiful but the workers are few (Matthew 9:37). We are here at this specific time for His eternal purposes (Acts 17:26-27). It's time to plant some seed!

PLANTING PLENTIFULLY

Sowing seed is the strategy of our Savior! Developing evangelistic methods, programs, and tools is important, but we should always do that in the context of sowing seed, not waiting for a perfect idea. Nothing compares to the value of just sowing seed and lots of it. We need to be intentional about sowing seed and persevering patiently as we do it (1 Corinthians 3:6-9).

PERSEVERING PATIENTLY

Sowing seed can be difficult and draining. Witnessing involves stepping into the firing squad of our enemy and the scorn of our society. The seed we sow will bear fruit, even in multiplicational ways, but that takes time. Staying close to Jesus and persevering patiently are vital (1 Corinthians 15:58).

We know exactly what needs to be done to advance the Gospel and fulfill the Great Commission. The question is will we do it? - David Jeremiah

---

We live in a world where millions of people have never heard or understood the Gospel. They won't be reached by Christians sitting around thinking about how to reach them. Believers need to join the Lord by participating purposefully, planting plentifully, and persevering patiently.

MAKING AN IMPACT

Have you ever found yourself stuck waiting for a perfect opportunity, a mystical prompting, a new tool, or for everything to feel just right? It's time to stop waiting. Ask God to show you any fear, insecurities, lies you've believed, or other things that stop you. Write those down along with the truth from God's Word that you will lean on when you next confront these obstacles?

DAY
TWENTY FOUR

1 Corinthians 3:6-15

I planted, Apollos watered, but God gave the growth. So then neither the one who plants nor the one who waters is anything, but only God who gives the growth. Now he who plants and he who waters are one, and each will receive his own reward according to his own labor. For we are God's coworkers. You are God's field, God's building. According to God's grace that was given to me, I have laid a foundation as a skilled master builder, and another builds on it. But each one is to be careful how he builds on it. For no one can lay any other foundation than what has been laid down. That foundation is Jesus Christ. If anyone builds on the foundation with gold, silver, costly stones, wood, hay, or straw, each one's work will become obvious. For the day will disclose it, because it will be revealed by fire; the fire will test the quality of each one's work. If anyone's work that he has built survives, he will receive a reward. If anyone's work is burned up, he will experience loss, but he himself will be saved — but only as through fire.

In the spring of 1976, my dad and a friend witnessed to a man named Tom Ray in front of the Too Bitter Bar in San Marcos, Texas. Tom was uninterested and continued on into the bar. Later that night, the band closed with, "I wish we'd all been ready," a Larry Norman song about the rapture. Tom knew God was trying to get his attention. Shortly later, in his lonely apartment, he put his trust in Christ. Tom has spent decades since as a pastor and has had a profound impact on my life for Christ. My dad could have easily left that conversation thinking it was a failure. It wasn't. God was working in Tom's life.

I know many other stories like this one. We don't always see immediate fruit but we can trust God will work if we simply obey. As we partner with the Lord, planting seed and watering it, He will produce eternally significant fruit.

PARTNERING WITH GOD IN HIS WORK

This passage calls us God's coworkers! Unbelievably, God chose you and me to be His hands, feet, and mouthpiece on earth. What an unparalleled privilege. What would you say if the president asked for your help on a project, or if a superstar athlete asked for your help preparing for a championship game? This is even bigger. The only sensible response is, "yes, I'm all in!" It is a joy to join Him, planting in His field!

PLANTING WITH GOD IN HIS FIELD

Yesterday's notes were all about planting seed. God's Word won't return void, and the Gospel always bears fruit (Isaiah 55:11 and Colossians 1:6). Even when we don't see immediate results, we can be confident that God will bring the fruit. All we need to do is to be obedient and press on with Him.

PRESSING ON WITH GOD UNTIL ETERNITY

Whether we see it or not, God will always produce fruit when we obey. All we need to do is to be patient and obedient, keeping our eyes on Him and eternity (2 Corinthians 4:17-18).

Evangelism is not an option for the Christian life. - Luis Palau

---

We have been called to partner with God in His work, to plant with God in His field, and to press on with God until eternity. There is no greater calling or honor in life.

MAKING AN IMPACT

Like I've said, sowing seed is more important than waiting for a perfect idea, method, or tool. That being said, every good farmer and diligent builder will use the tools of their trades for the work that they do. Today's passage tells us to plant and build wisely. Look at some of the resources in the back of this book and consider three you will try this week. List them below:

1. _____.

2. _____.

3. _____.

1 Peter 3:15

But in your hearts set apart Christ as Lord. Always be prepared to give an answer to everyone who asks you to give the reason for the hope that you have. But do this with gentleness and respect.

Have you ever been worried that someone would ask you a question you wouldn't be able to answer? That, it turns out, is a pervasive fear that keeps countless believers from sharing their faith. Never let it stop you again!

Many Christians are ignorant of basic apologetics, and some don't even know what the word means. The word apologetics comes from the Greek word ἀπολογία (pronounced apologia), translated here as, "to give an answer." The Greek word means, "a verbal defense." In other words, Christians are commanded to be able to defend their faith! This passage tells us to do that in a competent, caring, and Christ-focused way.

BEING COMPETENT

I've heard people say apologetics is worthless because, "if you can talk someone into our faith, they'll easily be talked out of it." That's nonsense. We all make important decisions based on the evaluation of evidence every day. Sharing the evidence for our faith in a way that emphasizes the Gospel in the power of the Holy Spirit is never in vain. Paul was committed to persuading people of the truth of the Gospel. We should be as well.

We all have apologetical homework to do. Just be careful; there are a plethora of terrible resources out there. Be careful to use good tools and training.

The BEST FACTS is a great tool. The BEST acronym stands for four great arguments for God's existence: the Beginning of the universe, the Engineering of the universe, Standards and morality, and the Truth about Jesus. The FACTS acronym stands for five great arguments for the trustworthiness of the Bible: it Foretells the future, is Archeologically accurate, is Coherent, is Translated correctly, and is full of Science that shows God's inspiration. Use these acronyms to defend your faith competently and remember to do that in a caring way.

Sound training in apologetics is one of the keys to fearless evangelism. - William Lane Craig

---

BEING CARING

As we competently share and defend our faith with a focus on Christ, we need to make sure to do it in a Christ-like way. Peter says to defend our faith with gentleness, meaning we should be loving, caring, and respectful as we proclaim Him to others. Don't blow your witness by treating someone disrespectfully.

BEING CHRIST-FOCUSED

This verse begins with Peter's challenge to, "set apart Christ as Lord." It concludes saying to defend our faith with respect (a Greek word meaning reverence and fear of God). Like Peter, Paul connects the fear God with persuading others about Him (2 Corinthians 5:11). When we correctly view God for who He is and acknowledge the truth of what He has told us in His Word, we won't neglect to share or defend our faith. Our relationship with the Lord is where evangelism and apologetics need to start (John 15:5).

Make the decision today to defend your faith in a competent, caring, and Christ-focused way.

MAKING AN IMPACT

Begin memorizing the BEST FACTS now so you'll be ready when the time comes. Visit thebestfacts.com for more information (don't forget to get the book and app while you're there). Spend a minute familiarizing yourself with the evidence for the resurrection (under the Truth about Jesus). Most Christians don't know this, but the evidence for the resurrection is irrefutable! Summarize some of what you find below so you'll be ready to share that when the topic comes up.

DAY
TWENTY SIX

Mark 13:10

And it is necessary that the Gospel be preached to all nations.

I have a close friend who I first met ministering in a closed country. He has spent decades since doing Christian work in a different area that is also restricted. Because of the nature of his work, he has to be very careful what he says and who he shares it with. As a consequence, few know of his ministry. He has spent years with almost no recognition for his work. He rarely gets to see friends and family in the United States. He often survives with minimal support. There have even been times when he has dealt with intense discouragement. He does what he does because he knows that the Gospel must be preached to all nations. His sacrificial service inspires me.

God wants every person alive to be saved (1 Timothy 2:4 and 2 Peter 3:9). He has always desired to be known among all the nations (Genesis 22:18 and Psalm 82:8). The time will come when that will be fulfilled. Scripture tells us brothers and sisters from every tribe, tongue, people, and nation will worship our Lord together in heaven (Revelation 5:9 and 7:9). That day is near.

That is why you are here today. God desires to use you to reach people He loves all across this planet, and His Holy Spirit is available to empower you for this (Acts 1:8). Jesus says that it is necessary that the Gospel be preached to all nations. That means that the Gospel must be preached, and the globe must be reached.

THE GOSPEL MUST BE PREACHED

The first part of this verse is powerful in and of itself: the Gospel must be preached! That's the truth, plain and simple. People will not be saved without hearing the Good News about Jesus (Acts 4:12 and Romans 10:13-15). We are His messengers. Most of this devotional has focused on that. Now I want to switch gears and talk about our role in fulfilling a global need.

THE GLOBE MUST BE REACHED

When Jesus says, "the Gospel must be preached to all nations," He uses a word we need to understand. The word nations, in this passage, comes from the Greek word ἔθνος (pronounced ethnos), which means "a race, tribe, nation, or ethnic group." It's the same word used in Matthew 28:19, when our Lord Himself tells us to, "Go, therefore, and make disciples of all nations." In other words, Jesus has given you and me the command to take the Gospel to and make disciples of every tribe, tongue, people, nation, and ethnic group.

You might be shocked to learn that there are more than half a million villages in India that know nothing about Jesus. When I first heard that, I cried like I hadn't in years. Did you know that only a tiny fraction of Christian donations and workers go to unreached people? We live in a time when unparalleled advances in communication, information, transportation, and other technologies have made reaching the whole world more possible than ever. Still, many of us have not taken the "all nations" part of the Great Commission seriously. The Gospel must be preached, and the globe must be reached.

Every Christian is either a missionary or an impostor. - Charles Spurgeon

---

MAKING AN IMPACT

You are a missionary. I believe your heart yearns to see people everywhere find our Savior. I want to challenge you to do three things to reach them.

1) **GIVE!** How is God calling you to support ministry to the unreached generously?

2) **GO!** How is God leading you to go on short or long term missions to unreached people, or serve with ministries that are going to them?

3) **GET ON YOUR KNEES!** How will you prioritize praying for unreached people and the workers going to them?

DAY
TWENTY SEVEN

Philippians 1:14 (NLT)

And because of my imprisonment, many of the Christians here have gained confidence and become more bold in telling others about Christ.

In the summer of 1973, my dad and a small group of traveling evangelists were arrested and thrown in jail for witnessing on the strip in front of the casinos in Las Vegas (he had a similar experience in Indianapolis). He said that nothing has ever made him feel closer to Christian brothers and sisters than experiencing a little persecution and taking communion together in jail. After the story broke on the news, many of the believers in the area rallied around the small group. After being released, their local outreaches began overflowing. God used the opposition they faced to expand their influence.

Many of us have never experienced anything like that. Still, we face difficulties every day, but often fail to recognize what God is doing in those inconveniences. Whether it's persecutions and imprisonments or problems and impediments, we need to acknowledge our obstacle, adjust our outlook, and act on our opportunities.

ACKNOWLEDGE YOUR OBSTACLE

Trials and inconveniences aren't always the real problems. God is working in each and every situation (Romans 8:28, Ephesians 1:11, and 2:10). The real obstacle is whatever keeps us from joining God in what He is doing all around us. That is often our unwillingness to submit our plans and expectations to His. Hebrews 12:1-2 tells us to get rid of our obstacles (our sin and hindrances), get on with our race, and get our eyes on Jesus. We need to do that with the biggest obstacle, our selfish perspective, and let Him adjust our outlook.

ADJUST YOUR OUTLOOK

Paul saw his imprisonment as a Gospel opportunity because that's how he approached everything in life. He had the same attitude in 1

Corinthians 9:12, saying that nothing, no right, no need, nor any inconvenience, would stop him from the work of the Gospel. He boldly stated that he would rather put up with anything than hinder the Gospel. What if we followed his example, and surrendered our rights, stayed the course, and sacrificed for God so that His work would be advanced, even at our expense? With that perspective, every circumstance could become an opportunity!

ACT ON YOUR OPPORTUNITY

We are called to make the most of every opportunity (Colossians 4:5). That includes all the different interruptions and crises we don't plan for or expect. The abundant life Jesus promised is not one of fulfilled expectations, but one of fulfilled purpose. Instead of letting our idea of a perfect life drive our choices, we can choose to let Christ and His Great Commission be our ambition, and trust Him to enable us to do His work in every circumstance, pleasant or not, that we encounter.

Paul never developed a negative attitude. He picked his bloody body up out of the dirt and went back into the city where he had almost been stoned to death, and he said, "Hey, about that sermon I didn't finish preaching - here it is!" - John Hagee

---

Our own self-centered worldview is usually our biggest obstacle. When we get that out of the way and allow God to adjust our outlook, we'll be ready to step through each new door He opens, whatever that might look like. When we do that, our examples will inspire others also!

MAKING AN IMPACT

Sometimes the most significant opportunities are disguised in the most frustrating circumstances. What if we were intentional about looking for those instead of becoming angry and frustrated when things don't unfold the way we hope they will? I imagine you have things that aren't going according to your plan right now. Ask God to show you how He is orchestrating those for His glory. Then, write down anything He shows you below, along with how you will point to Him in those trials.

_____

_____

_____

DAY
TWENTY EIGHT

Philippians 1:27-28 B

Just one thing: As citizens of heaven, live your life worthy of the Gospel of Christ. Then, whether I come and see you or am absent, I will hear about you that you are standing firm in one spirit, in one accord, contending together for the faith of the Gospel, not being frightened in any way by your opponents.

I don't know very many people more committed to sharing the Gospel than Don Cain. Even in his retirement, he makes time every week to be on campus sharing the Good News with young college students. He doesn't let insecurities or comfort zones keep him from the life and ministry God has called him to. He is also committed to helping other believers do the same. He is always discipling young men and taking them out witnessing. Don's life epitomizes the truths in today's passage.

Paul brought the Gospel to the Philippians, and his ministry grew into a vibrant body of believers in their city. Years later, he wrote to them from prison in Rome, expressing his desire that they would remain steadfast in all God had called them to. In today's short passage he encourages them that the Gospel should be lived out personally, that it should unite believers corporately, and that it should be expressed fearlessly.

THE GOSPEL SHOULD BE LIVED OUT PERSONALLY

Paul tells the Philippians to live their lives worthy of the Gospel of Christ. It's a lie that we have to be perfect to share our faith. God uses weak and broken sinners to show His power to the world (1 Corinthians 1:27-29). Still, we should be careful to follow Christ closely, obeying Him in the power of His Holy Spirit, so that others will see Him in us. You may have heard the saying that there are five Gospels, "Matthew, Mark, Luke, John, and your life." Although it sounds a little sacrilegious, there is a truth to it. We need to let Christ shine through us, and we need to join with other believers who do that too.

THE GOSPEL SHOULD UNITE BELIEVERS CORPORATELY

The Gospel is the cause that should align us! Very few things bring believers together like evangelism. It has fostered some of the closest relationships in my life, including friendships with many of the people I have mentioned already in this book, along with others, like my brother Dave, Tim Clemens, Craig Stirling, Russ Akins, John Ruppley, Darrell Dobbelmann, Jorge Hernandez, Michael Considine, Emray and Carol Goosen, and fellow GCA team members. When Christians contend together for the faith of the Gospel, they will always experience a deep sense of unity. That, in turn, becomes an encouragement when it comes to expressing the Gospel fearlessly.

THE GOSPEL SHOULD BE EXPRESSED FEARLESSLY

Paul challenged these Philippians to proclaim the Gospel, not being frightened in any way by their opponents. He had also shown them an example of this (Acts 16:12-40 and Philippians 1:14). We have been given the same charge by our Lord Himself (Matthew 5:14-16 and Acts 1:8).

If you had the cure to cancer wouldn't you share it? ... You have the cure to death ... get out there and share it. - Kirk Cameron

---

The Gospel should be lived out personally, it should unite believers corporately, and it should be expressed fearlessly. He has given us everything we need for that (2 Peter 1:3). Now, all we need to do is do it.

MAKING AN IMPACT

Earlier I talked about Don Cain's example of taking younger guys out witnessing. I also mentioned how Paul challenged the Philippians to share their faith together. I want to encourage you to start discipling younger believers and teaching them to share their faith. Our book Following Jesus: Discipleship Essentials is a great basic discipleship resource (order it on Amazon). Ask God who you should start discipling. Write their name below and then invite them to coffee and start working through the Following Jesus book together. The book will help you teach them to share their faith.

_____

_____

_____

DAY
TWENTY NINE

James 1:22 (NIV)

Do not merely listen to the Word, and so deceive yourselves. Do what it says.

Several years ago, I was leading an evangelism team at a major Christian music festival. One of my volunteers, Linda Roper, was significantly older than the rest and I wanted to be careful not to push her too hard. After sending everyone out in groups throughout the venue, I asked her if she would mind holding down the fort back at the evangelism team's tent. I figured she would appreciate having chairs, drinks, and a good view of the concert.

The next day she pulled me aside and gently told me, "If you want me back at the tent again that's fine, but I just thought I'd let you know I'd really appreciate it if you put me right down in the middle of the action." I soon came to find out that this sister takes the truth of God's Word seriously and puts it into practice sharing her faith boldly!

Authentic faith always motivates commitment and action. There are only three ways to respond to what we read in God's Word. We can arrogantly reject it, passively disregard it, or humbly apply it.

ARROGANTLY REJECTING GOD'S WORD

Those who reject the Lord and His Word are foolish indeed (Psalm 14:1 and 53:1). God forbid that Christians should ignore Him. God called those who refused to listen to His instruction false sons (Isaiah 30:9). Today's passage warns against hearing the Word and not doing what it says. That could involve those that arrogantly reject it or those who passively disregard it.

PASSIVELY DISREGARDING GOD'S WORD

Jesus was adamant that it is foolish to hear His Word and not put it into practice (Matthew 7:24-27). Unfortunately, many believers have settled into a comfortable Christianity that conveniently circumvents the difficult, challenging, or unpopular parts of the Bible. That often applies to evangelism, and that, according to today's passage, is why there is so much unbelief about witnessing.

"Not called!" did you say? "Not heard the call," I think you should say. Put your ear down to the Bible, and hear him bid you go and pull sinners out of the fire of sin. Put your ear down to the burdened, agonized heart of humanity, and listen to its pitiful wail for help. Go stand by the gates of hell, and hear the damned entreat you to go to their father's house and bid their brothers and sisters, and servants and masters not to come there. And then look Christ in the face, whose mercy you have professed to obey, and tell him whether you will join heart and soul and body and circumstances in the march to publish his mercy to the world. - William Booth

---

HUMBLY APPLYING GOD'S WORD

Knowledge without loving application always leads to arrogance and unbelief (1 Corinthians 8:1 and James 1:22). If we really believe God's Word, we will do what it says. Our actions are the ultimate evidence of our actual beliefs. True believers will always seek to humbly apply God's Word in the power of His Holy Spirit. That is true generally concerning Scripture; it is also true specifically concerning evangelism.

Truth unapplied always leads to deception. Because they have not obeyed the Word's instruction on evangelism, many have become filled with unbelief about the topic. We can arrogantly reject God's Word, passively disregard it, or humbly apply it. The wise will always do what it says.

MAKING AN IMPACT

If you really believe what you have spent the last month learning about in this devotional, you will put it into action. If you don't apply it, you will inevitably become filled with unbelief about evangelism. Review the past application sections. Are there any you skipped? Write them out below and refuse to let anything stop you from trusting God with those steps.

THIRTY

1 Corinthians 15:58

Therefore, my dear brothers and sisters, be steadfast, immovable, always excelling in the Lord's work, because you know that your labor in the Lord is not in vain.

Billy Graham spent seven decades in Christian work. During that time, millions of people came to Christ through his ministry. Over the years, he was asked to start his own university, host a television program, and even to run for president. He didn't let any of those possibilities distract him from his mission of sharing the Good News with the lost. He became an example of diligence, integrity, leadership, and commitment to the Lord and His work. He never lost his focus on evangelism. No one in recent times has demonstrated today's passage better.

You're probably familiar with the principle that "whenever you see a 'therefore,' you need to ask what it is there for." Well, this verse starts with a "Therefore," and it comes on the heels of Paul's conversation about Jesus' work at the Cross, His victory over sin and death, the reality of the resurrection and eternal life, and the proclamation of the Good News. In other words, because the Gospel is true, we should be steadfast, immovable, and always excelling in the Lord's work, knowing that our labor in the Lord is not in vain.

Since the Gospel is true, Paul says we should stand firm, serve fervently, and stay focused. We have the world's only true hope and all of eternity is on the line; how else could we respond?

STANDING FIRM

Paul says that believers are to be steadfast and immovable. We live in a world that is often critical of our message and opposed to our work. Many believers feel like school, work, and social expectations have silenced them. Others fear the backlash of a society that hates our Savior (Matthew 10:22, John 15:18, and 17:14). Still, Paul says, "stand firm and serve fervently!"

SERVING FERVENTLY

1 Corinthians 15:58 tells us to excel in the Lord's work; other translations say to abound in, be enthusiastic about, and give ourselves fully to His work. The point is obvious: we can't be half-hearted about Christ's mission of saving souls (Luke 19:10). We are to make known what He has done throughout the earth (Psalm 105:1), and we are to do that with an obedient, passionate, committed, and diligent focus.

STAYING FOCUSED

We can't be apathetic. If we love Him and the lost we will stay locked in on His Great Commission, knowing that our labor is never in vain. It is a privilege and unparalleled joy to follow Him on this mission. John the Baptist didn't consider himself worthy to untie our Lord's sandals (Matthew 3:11, Mark 1:7, Luke 3:16, John 1:27, and Acts 13:25). The apostles were amazed that God counted them worthy of being persecuted for Christ (Acts 5:41). Paul considered all his greatest accolades and achievements as garbage compared to knowing Him (Philippians 3:7-11). How could we ever begrudge His call to evangelism? It is an honor to join Him in His work as His co-laborers (1 Corinthians 3:9).

Can we be casual in the work of God - casual when the house is on fire, and people in danger of being burned? - Duncan Campbell

---

The message in today's scripture is clear: the truth of the Gospel compels a response. If we really believe what we say we believe, we will stand firm, serve fervently, and stay focused on His work!

MAKING AN IMPACT

We've spent the last month together, digging deep into passage after passage on witnessing. After all you've learned, I don't want you to fall into the sin of omission concerning evangelism. Go back to the application section on day twenty-two. I asked you to write down the names of a few evangelistic friends. I want you to take that a step further. Ask one of them to keep you accountable to these things. Write their name down below and make a plan to catch up on this every so often.

THIRTY ONE

Matthew 25:21

His master said to him, "Well done, good and faithful servant! You were faithful over a few things; I will put you in charge of many things. Share your master's joy."

Imagine you are standing in front of Jesus, seeing Him eye to eye for the first time. Billions are worshipping Him all around you. Everything about this place is more extravagant than anything you had ever imagined. You sense peace, joy, and satisfaction in a way that surpasses anything you ever experienced on earth. This is wonderful. Words don't begin to describe it. You are exhilarated to be here, but surprised it happened so soon. Your life on earth is but a memory. You are here now.

As you stand in sheer amazement and awe, Jesus, Lord and Savior, God and Creator, the One who died for you and rose again so you could be in this place, looks you straight in the eyes and says, "Well done, good and faithful servant!" From this vantage point, every risk, trial, and sacrifice you endured on earth for Him seems trivial. You lived your life focused on your Savior, His work, and this day. Now you are here. It was all worth it!

Sometimes it seems too good to be true, but make no mistake about it, the day will come when you and I will stand before Jesus! Today's verse comes from a longer parable, in Matthew 25:14-30, that appears in an extended context of Christ's return. We don't know when we will see Him face to face, but we will. Today's parable reminds us to live with that day in mind, accepting responsibility, actively investing, and aiming for eternity.

WE MUST ACCEPT RESPONSIBILITY

Jesus told us that the Gospel must be preached to all nations (Mark 13:10). He called His followers to be fishers of people (Matthew 4:19). He gave us the charge to shine brightly in this world (Matthew 5:14-16). He empowers us with His Spirit to be His witnesses to the ends of the earth (Acts 1:8). We can shrug all of that off, believing the lie that it's for superstar Christians, or, we can accept responsibility and enthusiastically follow Him in the adventure and destiny we were made for. I beg you, accept responsibility and invest in eternity. You will never regret it.

WE MUST ACTIVELY INVEST

We can either bury the talents He has given us or make the most of them, in His power. Jesus tells us to store up treasure in heaven, not on earth (Matthew 6:19-21). Paul was adamant about the importance of investing in eternity (1 Corinthians 3:10-15). God has endowed you with abilities and resources to be used for His Great Commission! Don't bury those in earthly interests and possessions; invest them in eternity.

WE MUST AIM FOR ETERNITY

Whatever you sacrifice for the Lord today will be well worth it. Remember, "our momentary light affliction is producing for us an absolutely incomparable eternal weight of glory. So we do not focus on what is seen, but on what is unseen. For what is seen is temporary, but what is unseen is eternal" (2 Corinthians 4:17-18). We have been given a trust, and we must be faithful with it (1 Corinthians 4:2). We need to make the most of every opportunity for the Lord (Colossians 4:5).

> "Three-hundred-million years from now, the only thing that will matter is who is in heaven and who is in hell. And if that is the only thing that will matter then, that should be one of our greatest concerns now." - Mark Cahill

---

You are alive today according to God's plan. Please, take what you have learned this past month and apply it. Make the impact you were made to accomplish. You don't have what it takes, but the Holy Spirit in you does!

MAKING AN IMPACT

Jesus gave us a Great Commission to complete (Matthew 28:18-20)! I can't wait to share stories of what He did in and through us when we see each other in heaven. I challenge you, live this life with that in mind. Turn the page to the closing challenge and prayerfully ask the Lord how He would have you respond!

A CONCLUDING
CHALLENGE

Congratulations! You've just finished a full month of evangelism training! Thank you so much for working through this devotional. I hope God used it in your life. Take a minute to reflect on all God has taught you this past month. Then, on the following pages, write a personal charter that outlines how you want to live the rest of your life implementing these truths in the power of the Holy Spirit.

A NOTE TO
LEADERS

2 Timothy 4:5

But as for you, exercise self-control in everything, endure hardship, do the work of an evangelist, fulfill your ministry.

The Church needs godly leaders in a desperate way. If we are ever going to reach our world for Christ, Christian leaders need to be willing to lead by example when it comes to evangelism.

Jesus led by example (Matthew 20:25-28 and John 13:1-17). Paul led by example (1 Corinthians 11:1). Paul told Timothy to lead by example too (1 Timothy 4:12). We need to lead by example as well. Leading by example is critical. Paul knew that un-evangelistic leaders would inevitably multiply un-evangelistic followers. That is why he told Timothy to do the work of an evangelist.

To call a man evangelical who is not evangelistic is an utter contradiction. - G. Campbell Morgan

---

Whether it is your primary gift or not, you need to be sharing your faith if you are a leader. The people you lead need to see you trust God with your fears and share your faith. They need to hear your stories and receive your encouragement. If you commit to sharing your faith often, your example will inspire your congregation. A ministry that loves the Lord and reaches out to the lost will be one that is constantly thriving and growing. But, no group will get to that place if they don't see their leaders' examples.

You will create a culture of unbelief about evangelism if you don't share your faith, or if you leave that for others in the church, or if you say things like, "my job inside these four walls is to teach you so you can go outside of them." The result of that kind of apathetic leadership will be a church that doesn't care about the lost. You'll soon find that is a discouraging group of people to work with.

At the end of the day, leaders who don't obey God's Word do more harm than good. Leaders who are unwilling to share their faith should not lead. Otherwise, they'll be leading others into sin. Remember, leaders will give an account for how they lead (Hebrews 13:17), and teachers will give an account for how they teach (James 3:1).

Friend, I want to encourage you to lead by example in the area of evangelism. Those you lead need you to do this for them. If you need help, the GCA team is here to support you in this. Pick up our book Great Commission Leadership on Amazon and visit the GCA site at greatcommissionalliance.org for more resources. Contact us if you'd like us to come alongside you to help you and your church. We're here for you.

Jesus wants to use you and your ministry in great evangelistic ways. As you share your faith, and teach others to also, you will be leading the way God calls you to by setting an example for those you lead.

EVANGELISM
RESOURCES AND IDEAS

The following few pages will give you a few evangelism techniques and tools that I believe will prove very useful. You can also get more training and resources at:

greatcommissionalliance.org/evangelismresources

Finally, please pick up my book titled 101 Easy, Effective, and Exciting Evangelism Ideas on Amazon for even more ideas.

THE SHARE ACRONYM

This strategy is a simple way of remembering an effective approach to personal evangelism. SHARE stands for Supercharge, Have an expectant attitude, Ask questions, Resources, and Encourage them. Let's get into each of those issues a little more in depth.

Supercharge

Acts 1:8 tells us that the Holy Spirit empowers us for bold evangelism. Remember the POWER acronym? It will remind you how to walk in the Holy Spirit's power when you're witnessing. Here is how you can walk in the power of the Holy Spirit each day.

Present yourself to God, surrendering to Him to be used in evangelism (Romans 12:1-2).

Own up to any sin He makes you aware of in this area and confess it to Him; He will forgive you (1 John 1:9).

Want to honor God as His witness, choosing to live a Spirit-filled and empowered life (Matthew 5:6).

Experience His power for evangelism by asking Him to fill you with His Spirit and believing He will by faith (James 1:6-7 and 1 John 5:14-15).

Rely on Him, taking a step of faith to share your faith and trusting He will empower you for that (2 Corinthians 5:7).
Before witnessing, consciously ask God to fill you with His Holy Spirit, empowering you to witness with His power and authority. Pray

for those you will share with (remember the "Divine Order"). Then step out, supercharged with His power, trusting Him to work in other peoples' lives through you.

Have an expectant attitude

Look for opportunities and expect God to use you in great ways! Do not share your faith with a "no one will be interested, no one will respond, no one wants to hear this" attitude. Go out excited to see all God will do! Your attitude will affect your willingness to obey God, the frequency with which you obey Him, the way you come across to those you share with, and every other aspect of evangelism. Determine today to share your faith with a joyful and expectant attitude.

Ask questions

You can transition any conversation to the Gospel in simple and non-awkward ways, and questions are the key to doing that! Think of a few conversation-starting questions you could use to get into conversations with people. Then, think of a good question that can transition to a conversation about Christ. A great example is, "What's been your experience with Christianity?" It is vitally important that you make questions a key component of your evangelism strategy.

Resources

Use resources that will help you confidently share your faith and train the next generation of people you're discipling to as well. We call these transferable resources. A great example is the KGP (Knowing God Personally) booklet, available from Cru (or with the God Tools app).

Gospel presentations like this are conversational tools that help millions of people each year put their faith in Christ. Don't shun such powerful and transferable tools, just learn how to use them in relational and non-awkward ways. Another great resource for evangelism is your personal testimony. There will be more on that in just a minute.

Encourage them

Be ready to implement a follow-up plan right away. Whether someone puts their trust in Christ or is interested in hearing more, plan to meet up with them again to encourage them towards Christ. Get their contact information before leaving and don't delay in setting up a follow-up appointment. It is a shame how many hungry seekers are never followed up with, and it is just as tragic when new believers are not discipled. Don't make either of these mistakes!

So there you have it, the SHARE acronym. If you will supercharge before witnessing, going out in the power of the Holy Spirit rather than your own abilities, you will see fruit in evangelism. If you have an expectant attitude, you'll have tremendous joy in witnessing and will see God use you in greater ways than you can imagine. If you learn to ask questions in evangelistic conversations, you'll find yourself transitioning all sorts of conversations to the Gospel. Remember to listen carefully and show people you love them when you do this. If you add resources to all that, you'll be powerfully equipped to share your faith anytime and anywhere with anyone. Finally, if you encourage those you share with, following up with those who are interested, and discipling those who put their trust in Christ, you will see a constant flow of new believers flowing from your ministry. Implement this SHARE acronym in your life and ministry, and you won't believe all God will do in and through you.

USE YOUR TESTIMONY TO SHARE THE GOSPEL

Your personal testimony is a powerful tool. Go ahead and carefully put together your personal testimony, the story of what God has done in your life, using this shortened version of the One Minute Witness from Oasis World Ministries. Read through each section (part A, B, C, and D) and then write out your answers on the next page in one complete section.

PART A: What three words described your life before Christ? If you trusted Christ at a young age, describe three aspects of your sinful nature apart from Christ.

Start this with, "There was a time in my life when," and then complete the sentence with the three things that used to define you.

Complete **PART A** on page 79.

PART B: How did you come to faith in Christ? Include the details of how you put your faith in Christ and briefly describe the key aspects of the Gospel here (God's love, your sin, Jesus' provision, and your decision to trust Him).

Continue with, "And then one day," (then explain how you heard and understood the Gospel; summarize the Gospel there). Then add, "When I realized what Jesus had done for me, I" (explain how you responded to the Gospel).

Complete **PART B** below.

PART C: What three words describe your life after Christ?

Start this with, "Since I've met Jesus, He has changed me and now I am," and then complete the sentence with the three things that describe how He has changed you.

Complete **PART C** on page 80.

PART D: Summarize your story with a sentence. Begin that sentence with, "If I had never met Jesus," then explain what that would look like; end the sentence with, "but because of Him..." Then, ask the person you're talking with if they'd like to know how Jesus could do something like this in their life.

Complete **PART D** on page 80.

Write your testimony here:

Complete part A: "There was a time in my life when, _____, _____, and _____ defined who I was.

Complete part B:

And then one day,

When I realized what Jesus had done for me, I

Complete part C: Since I've met Jesus, He has changed me and now I am _____, _____, and _____.

Complete part D:

If I had never met Jesus:

but because of Him:

Then ask, "would you like to know how Jesus could do something like this in your life?"

Personalize, develop and refine this. Keep it simple and Christ-focused (1 Corinthians 2:1–2). Try keeping it to a minute. Practice it and be ready to share it often! You can also initiate a conversation by asking someone if you can ask them a question. If they say, "yes," ask, "What is the greatest thing that has ever happened to you?" Listen to them, show them you care, and then ask if you can share the greatest thing that has ever happened to you. If they say yes, share your testimony. God will use you!

MEET NEW PEOPLE AND SHARE THE GOSPEL WITH THEM

Continually meeting new people is vitally important if you are going to reach the world for Christ. The second you stop meeting new people your ministry and influence die. Meeting people is the first step in sharing the Gospel. There are a few great ways to meet new people anywhere and anytime. You can share the Gospel with anyone you cross paths with if you'll apply these ideas for meeting people and then work through the sound barriers we'll discuss after this.

The REACH acronym will remind you of five great ways to meet new people in virtually any context. Even if you aren't an extrovert, you can learn to be good at meeting people (and the Holy Spirit inside you is more than capable). Each part of the REACH acronym is described below.

Relate

Smile, wave, introduce yourself, etc. The longer you wait, the more awkward it will get. Make it a point to be friendly and open with people the second you meet them. This will open up countless opportunities for evangelism.

Environment

Get out of your comfort zones. Get involved in groups where you will be forced to meet new people (great places to meet people include sports, hobbies, classes, ministry events like concerts, etc.). Look for conversation starters around you wherever you happen to be. Try to begin a conversation based on the person's clothes or possessions (for example, if they're wearing an Alaska T-shirt, ask "Where have you been in Alaska?"). Try to begin a conversation based on something from your surroundings (for example, if your standing in line with someone, say, "This is quite a line, huh?"). Try to begin a conversation based on something in the media (news, entertainment, sports, politics, etc., are all great conversation starters). Finally, try to begin a conversation based on a shared circumstance (for example, ask, "What movies would you suggest I watch?").

Ask questions

People rarely sense others are genuinely interested in them, so be genuinely interested in them. Ask lots of questions. Keep it appropriate. Ask open-ended, conversation promoting questions. Refrain from questions with "yes" or "no" answers (for example, asking "What's the best thing on the menu" is much better than asking, "is the food here good?"). Ask good follow up questions to their answers. Ask and then listen! Listen carefully and show you care.

Compliment someone

Start a conversation by complimenting someone. Be careful, appropriate, and honest. An authentic compliment is always a great way to meet someone.

Help

Help someone that needs help or ask for help from a stranger if you need help. Helping someone who needs it and asking someone for help both create a natural opportunity to meet people.

Take the initiative in the power of the Holy Spirit! The Great Commission starts with "Go." We can't sit around and wait, but must go and meet new people where they are at. Then, we can transition those conversations to the Gospel.

TRANSITION ANY CONVERSATION TO THE GOSPEL

Sharing the gospel involves breaking through four different "sound barriers." This concept was developed by Keith Davy with Cru. These stages are called sound barriers because each involves a barrier where sound must come from your mouth! Each barrier represents a real point in every conversation where you will be tempted to give in to fear and back down. It is vitally important to analyze where you are at in a conversation and trust Jesus and His Spirit in you to cross the next sound barrier. Trusting Him is the foundation. Understand these barriers but go in a context of prayer, filled and controlled by His Spirit. Then, cross each of these barriers by faith!

Sound Barrier #1.

Meeting someone and initiating a conversation. This can be done in a natural way (remember the REACH acronym we just reviewed). After meeting someone, keep asking questions to keep the conversation going. Practice meeting new people and getting conversations going.

Sound Barrier #2.

Moving from a general conversation to a spiritual conversation. Once you are talking with someone about general topics (the weather, news, hobbies, etc.), it is easy to transition to a spiritual conversation by asking thoughtful questions. For example, if you are talking about the news and all the bad in the world, you could easily ask what their hope is in. Keep asking questions that will transition to a spiritual conversation.

Sound Barrier #3.

Moving from a spiritual conversation to the Gospel. From a spiritual conversation, you can easily transition to the Gospel by asking another transition question like, "what has been your experience with Christianity?" From there it is very easy to continue into a presentation of the Gospel. Make sure to include all the necessary aspects of the Gospel in your presentation. A great way to do this is to use a Gospel tract as a conversational tool.

Sound Barrier #4.

Moving from the gospel to a decision. No presentation of the gospel is complete without asking the person you are witnessing to to respond to Christ's message. Most good tools will include this (for example, Cru's "Know God Personally" booklet concludes by asking the person where they're at and where they'd like to be, and then telling them how to get there). Whatever tool or method you use, make sure to convey the fact that they have a decision to make.

Those are the four barriers. They provide a great way to transition any conversation to the Gospel. As you seek to transition your conversations to the Gospel, consider what it is you find yourself talking about most often. You could even use the topics you listed on day fifteen. Come up with good transition questions for those topics.

This concept will help you transition any conversation to the Gospel. Understanding the four sound barriers will also help you evaluate your evangelistic conversations to see where you are falling short (you can evaluate every gospel presentation by asking yourself how many barriers you got through). Take a step of faith and trust God to help you transition each conversation to the Gospel! If you practice working through each of these barriers, you will quickly find yourself sharing the Gospel fearlessly and often!

USE A TRANSFERABLE CONVERSATIONAL TOOL TO SHARE THE GOSPEL

Some say that these evangelistic tools no longer work; that's probably because they've never used them. The Gospel is the power of God (Rom. 1:16) regardless of what format you present it in. Good tools are helpful in sharing your faith. Cru's "Know God Personally," or KGP booklet is a great way to go.

These tools should include a simple but complete summary of the gospel. They can be great conversation starters. You can ask, "Have you ever seen the 'name of the tool you are using,'" (for example, the Knowing God Personally booklet)? You can show a person how to receive Christ in a short period of time. Most of these tools begin with a high point, God's love. They should clearly present how to receive Christ. They build confidence (you know what you're going to say before you say it). And most importantly, they are a transferable method for teaching others to witness. Anyone can use them.

When you use evangelistic tools, personalize them to make them less "canned." Avoid a lifeless approach by reading, then illustrating and finally personalizing what you share. When using the KGP or similar evangelistic presentations remember the following guidelines. Expose the Gospel, don't impose on the person. Go in love, in the power and direction of the Holy Spirit; make sure Christ is on the throne. Pray, remembering the "Divine Order." You are called to present the gospel clearly in the power of the Holy Spirit. Trust God with the results. Always present the opportunity for a response but don't force it. Without an adequate understanding of the Gospel, there can't be a legitimate response.

You can get the print versions of these tools or get the God Tools app for your phone. I know using a good Gospel conversational tool will help you accurately communicate the whole Gospel each time you share while doing it in a way that anyone who happens to be with you could do as well. You can never have too many tools!

SHARE JESUS WITHOUT FEAR

William Fay's book, Share Jesus Without Fear, describes another great approach to conversational evangelism. He describes five questions which can be introduced to any conversation to transition to the Gospel. Question one is, "Do you have any kind of spiritual beliefs?" Question two is, "To you, who is Jesus Christ?" Question three is, "Do you think there is a heaven or hell?" Question four is, "If you died, where would you go?" If they say heaven, you can ask, "why?" Finally, question five is, "If what you are believing is not true would you want to know?" These questions provide an easy way for someone to bring any conversation to a spiritual one and an opportunity to introduce Christ and His offer of a gift of salvation to all that put their trust in Him.

Once the conversation has turned in a spiritual direction, seven scriptures can be shared with the hearer. Invite the person to read each out loud from your Bible. Fay uses this technique trusting the power of God's Word to draw people to Him (remember Romans 10:17). These verses are Romans 3:23, Romans 6:23, John 3:3, John 14:6, Romans 10:9-11, 2 Corinthians 5:15 and Revelation 3:20. Ask the person you are sharing with what they think each verse means after finishing reading it and before continuing to the next verse.

Fay encourages his readers to bring every conversation to a point of decision before concluding, and once again, he gives five great questions to help with this. They are: 1) Are you a sinner? 2) Do you want forgiveness of sins? 3) Do you believe Jesus died on the cross for you and rose again? 4) Are you willing to surrender your life to Jesus

Christ? 5) Are you ready to invite Jesus into your life and into your heart? These questions help bring a person to a point of decision. If they are ready to put their trust in Christ, you can lead them to do that through prayer.

USE THE SOULARIUM TO INITIATE GOSPEL CONVERSATIONS

The Soularium tool, from Cru, is one of the greatest tools I've ever found. You can use this tool conversationally by just walking up to strangers and asking, "Have you ever seen the Soularium before?" They'll usually say, "no, what is it?" You can tell them it is a picture survey about life's biggest questions. I always mention that it is a creative way for the listener to share their views with me. This tool completely disarms people and destroys walls. I've had people tell me, within minutes of meeting them, "I want to be pure again but I don't know how," "I am searching," "I feel like everything around me is dark and I know the light is out there, I am looking but haven't found it yet," "I want my soul to go up (to heaven)," "I feel like I am rusted out, falling apart, broken, and I need someone to come and help me" and other similar comments. If you think it would be great having people open up like that within moments of meeting them, you need to get your hands on this tool and use it often. You can get the app in the app stores or just search Soularium by Cru to find where you can buy it online.

USE THE PERSPECTIVE CARDS TO SHARE THE GOSPEL

Yet another great tool from CRU! The perspective cards ask 1) what is the nature of God, 2) what is human nature, 3) what is life's purpose, 4) who is Jesus and 5) what is the source of truth. For each of those questions, there are a number of cards, each with a perspective common today. After the person you are talking with shares their perspective, you have the opportunity to share the Biblical perspective on each of those topics. It ends up being a great way to get into deep spiritual conversations and share the Good News in a relatively short period of time. You can also get these in banner form, which is a great resource for churches and ministries. Get the perspectives app in the app stores or just search Perspectives by Cru to find where you can buy it online.

USE GOOD EVANGELISM APPS

There are numerous evangelism apps that you can get for free, that will help you share the Gospel confidently. One essential evangelism app is Cru's God Tools app. This app includes multiple Gospel presentation conversation tools along with Cru's Holy Spirit booklet and a link to everystudent.com, a site full of apologetics and evangelistic articles and Q&As. This app will equip you to share the Gospel clearly whenever and wherever you happen to be. Don't forget the Soularium and Perspectives apps either. You should also pick up the Share Jesus without Fear app. Don't be caught dead without some of these great apps on your phone, tablet, or other devices. Don't just download them and leave them either. Practice using these tools to meet people and share the Gospel with them.

USE TRACTS TO SHARE THE GOSPEL

Some people would say these don't work any longer. They may not be as effective as they once were but it is crazy to write them off. I have a pastor friend who came to Christ by grabbing a tract off the top of a trash can. I have another ministry friend who came to Christ after coming across a tract while attempting suicide. Make it a point to get some good, unique, trendy tracts that you can distribute in creative ways. Don't be awkward about it but don't miss this great opportunity either. You can get tracts at various sites online.

SHARE AN EVANGELISTIC WEBSITE

Here's the simplest idea for sharing your faith you will probably ever hear. Share an evangelistic website with your friends and post it to your social networks. Several ministries focus completely on reaching people through the web. These typically reach thousands daily with the Gospel. So here is the idea: think through any friends you have that don't yet know Jesus and send them a message encouraging them to check out one of the following sites. If the person is a college student send them to everystudent.com (this is geared towards students, but this site is good for anyone who might be interested in spiritual things). Send others to lookingforgod.com. Other great links include istheremoretolife.com and viewthestory.com (which allows you to create a customized account and link for your friends). You should also post these links to your Facebook, Twitter or other social media with a short message like, "want to know more about Jesus, click here."

If you think these sites are irrelevant, think again; as I write, this afternoon, over 74,000 people have indicated decisions to trust in Christ on everystudent.com and other Global Media Outreach sites (you can see live stats at greatcommission2020.com). You never know, one of those live decisions for Christ might end up being one of your friends (if you share these evangelistic links that is)! And, in case you were wondering, these decisions aren't just random numbers out in internet land. They are real people, and real believers really follow up with them. You could even help with that by visiting globalmediaoutreach.com. Finally, don't forget to pray for these people as you watch these live decisions for Christ and don't forget to share these sites with friends and on your networks. Seriously, could evangelism get any simpler?

USE SOMEONE'S NAME TO TRANSITION TO THE GOSPEL

What's in a name? An opportunity to share the Gospel! Seriously, every name presents an opportunity for the Gospel. This evangelism idea is so easy, and it is a great way to get started working through the sound barriers! Simply ask someone you meet what their name is. Then, quickly, try to think of someone that has influenced you for Christ with that same name. Tell your new friend you have a friend with their same name. Then, continue describing who that friend is and what their influence on you has been. This friend could be a pastor, mentor, encourager or just a friend from church. The bottom line is that as soon as you tell them about this friend and their influence on you, you can begin transitioning into a conversation about Christ by asking what their experience has been with Christianity.

ASK ABOUT CHURCH

This has got to be one of my all-time favorite, easiest imaginable ways to get into evangelistic conversations. It always works. This is the idea I was using in the story from the devotional on day two. Next time you're out of town, ask someone (at a gas station, hotel, restaurant or wherever you happen to be) what the church scene is like in that city. Whether they're a believer or not, that will instantly begin a conversation about Christianity which can easily be transitioned back to the Gospel. I really hope you get a chance to try it out!

ASK SOMEONE ABOUT THEIR WEEKEND

This is a super easy, "throwing out the line" idea that you can try this coming Monday. It will work best with people you've never discussed your faith with before. Start out by asking people you see Monday what they did this weekend. Then listen. When they are done telling you about their weekend, they will probably ask you the same thing. When they do, tell them your weekend was great and mention that you had a great time at church (this is the "throwing out the line" component, pray they bite). You could also mention something other than church as long as you can relate it to God (for example, a retreat, a Christian book you read, etc.). Then ask them if they have any kind of background in Christianity or church. The second you ask "what did you do last weekend," you open up a conversation that will quickly and easily go towards the Gospel. As you throw out the line and then continue with your answer when they ask you, you are respectfully giving them an opportunity to "bite." Good chance they will.

No matter where they are at with Jesus, invite them to your church next week. Just a quick note on that, inviting someone to church doesn't replace evangelism (you should never do this instead of sharing the Gospel), but it is a friendly gesture and you'll be surprised how often people will take you up on it.

TELL SOMEONE HOW GOD CAME THROUGH FOR YOU

Years ago, we fought our insurance company for sixteen weeks about payment for our second daughter's delivery. They were legally required to pay the $19,000 bill but initially rejected it. We waited forever for their review, which we finally received, finding it had been denied. I asked our prayer team to pray God would change their minds. Three hours after I sent out that e-mail, I got a call from the main lady overseeing our review. She said she was sorry for overlooking something and said, "disregard the denial we sent you, we have paid this bill." We ended up fighting them for nearly another year to make sure they paid the whole bill but were still amazed by the miracle God pulled off (we also switched to Samaritan Ministries, a health sharing ministry after that debacle). Bottom line, God came through for us!

That brings me to the next evangelism idea: tell a non-Christian, in your sphere of influence, something amazing your Father has done in your life in the last couple of weeks. Brag on God. He is your heavenly Father and the source of every good thing you have (James 1:17). Talk freely about what He has done for you and all you have to be thankful for. This will lead to an obvious opportunity for you to bring up the Gospel. Next time you find yourself in a conversation with someone you want to share with, simply share a story of God's faithfulness and then get to the Gospel from there. I hope you have a blast telling others about what God has done in your life and I hope you get to share the Gospel in every one of those conversations.

TELL SOMEONE ABOUT THE STRUGGLES YOUR TRUSTING GOD WITH

Don't hide the hard times you're going through, allow God to use even those for His glory! I've watched Christian friends go through many of the toughest things you could ever imagine, trusting Christ through it all, and shining brighter in that darkness than ever before. Demonstrating hope in difficult situations often leads to opportunities for evangelism. Why not try this idea instead of getting frustrated the next time you are faced with a trial (and remember Romans 8:28 and James 1:2-4). I am sure God will do great things in and through you as you trust Him!

INVITE SOMEONE TO CHURCH

This idea is simple and just takes a little initiative: invite people to church! Dr. Thom Rainer says that "82% of the unchurched are at least somewhat likely to attend church if invited." That stat blows my mind! Why aren't we inviting everyone we meet to church? Nobody will kill you for asking. I imagine many of the people you find in your sphere of influence would probably come if invited. Even if they don't, it will bring up a great spiritual conversation (you could ask them what their experience with church has been).

If they do join you, remember it doesn't end there! After church, don't assume they're good to go. You will need to clarify the Gospel. You could buy them lunch and ask good questions over lunch. You could ask, "What stuck out most to you from the service today," or, "What did you think when the pastor said..." These questions will bring up a great conversation, and if you are intentional, you will be able to share the Gospel with them.

TELL SOMEONE JESUS LOVES THEM

Telling someone that Jesus loves them is a great way to share the Gospel. This works great in situations where you only have a few moments. You could do this at grocery stores as you check out, at gas stations, or anywhere else you make a purchase or have a brief encounter with someone. Simply ask, "When was the last time someone told you that Jesus loves you?" Then wait for their response. Whatever they say, make sure to let them know He really does love them.

I've had so many interesting responses to this. Once a man told me, "God hates me." That obviously opened up into a great evangelistic conversation. Another time I did this, the lady broke into tears explaining how just a few hours earlier her husband had dropped all of her belongings off at the store and told her not to come home. I was able to share the Gospel with her, and she indicated a desire to put her trust in Christ. Another time I did this the clerk told me, "Scram!" That's the only negative response I've ever had though.

Why don't you give it a shot and then look for an opportunity to share the Gospel once you're talking with the person! Even if you don't get to share more, trust God will use the little you did get to communicate to impact them.

ASK SOMEONE IF YOU CAN PRAY FOR THEM

Here is another story as told by my friend Austin Krokos, one of the most gifted evangelists I know. He writes:

I was talking to my friend yesterday about money issues. He said he was bummed that he had a dental disease that would cost him $4,000 to fix, but he was in the process of buying a house and could not afford both. I asked, "Wow, can I pray for you right now," He said, "yes," and we bowed our heads for a thirty minute prayer. Afterwards, he said, "thanks, I pray sometimes, but feel like I am asking for too much for myself." I was able to share scripture with him, specifically times Jesus tells us to ask Him for things. Then I asked if he had a relationship with God, or if it was something he was working on? He said he was working on it. I asked if he was willing to check out a booklet that summarized what a relationship with God began with, He said, "yes." I was able to share the Gospel with him.

I once did this with a self-proclaiming atheist. He said, "yes," and I was able to pray with him and share the Gospel with him. A short time later he publicly stated that he had put his faith in Christ. This is a great idea, and it is so simple. Next time you have an opportunity, ask someone if you can pray for them, then, trust God to give you an opportunity to share the Good News with them.

SHARE THE NEXT TIME YOU EAT OUT

One way to share the next time you eat out is to ask the person serving you if they have a prayer need. My former Pastor, Erik Christiansen, told me about this one. Simply tell your server that you like to pray before you eat and then ask if they have anything you could pray for them about. You'll be surprised how many will take you up on the offer. Then, be ready to keep a Gospel conversation going afterwards, if time permits. Just make sure to respect their work schedule.

Another way to witness is to tip well and leave a Gospel focused note. Unfortunately, Christians are known for being terrible tippers (I have known Christian waitresses who have told me that this is common knowledge in the restaurant industry). Erin and I have always tried to tip our servers more than they would ever expect and we always leave a short message on the tip telling them about Jesus (we usually write it on the receipt)! I have had waitresses tell me how much those messages mean to them and have even been able to pray with them before. If you eat out often at a certain location, you will soon develop a very good reputation and a very godly witness.

SHARE A GOOD BOOK

We all have non-Christian friends, relatives, neighbors, co-workers, and relatives we want to share the Good News with. One way to share with them is to give them a good book. Of course, the best book you could ever give them is the Bible. Even if they aren't a believer, you can buy them a high quality gift Bible that would look nice on any bookshelf and would be there the next time they became interested in investigating further. Find a book that would be aimed at their level and likely to answer some of the spiritual questions they have (something like The Case for Christ would be a great idea). This would be a great idea for a gift as well. You might want to buy a stash of ten or twenty to keep on hand for whenever you have an opportunity to give one away. I just bought ten copies of I Don't Have Enough Faith to be an Atheist to hand out. I hope this simple idea opens up a ton of doors for you to share your faith!

BUY A LOTTERY TICKET

I do hope you'll take a gamble on this idea. I strongly encourage you not to take up gambling of any other sort, including buying lottery tickets, with just this one exception. This idea came to Austin Krokos and I late one night at a gas station. Purchase a lottery ticket from a cashier and ask him what the current lottery winnings are projected to be. Then ask him how his life would change if he won that much money. Listen to his answer and then give him the ticket and tell him you hope he wins it all. Then ask if you can share something else even more valuable with him. He probably won't turn you down. If there is time, go ahead and share the Gospel with him, if not, leave him a tract. Either way, you will have just managed to share the Gospel in a very unique and creative way for just a couple of bucks. Good chance the employee will tell others about the whole thing as well.

DO SOME GARAGE SALE EVANGELISM

This idea is unbelievably simple and effective. Coordinate a garage sale, get together a bunch of stuff you want to sell, and then advertise it. You might invite your neighbors to join you as well. Don't forget to take the initiative to share with them as you spend the day with them. Put out a box or a table with a bunch of New Testaments, other Bibles, and tracts on top of it. Then, put a large note across the front that says, "Free Bibles." Ask each customer if you can give them a free Bible (include a tract with it if they say yes). You'll find very few will turn you down, and it will open up evangelistic conversations with many! You'll also make some money on the side which might make this one of the most lucrative evangelism ideas (not that you'd ever do it for that reason).

Well, there are a few practical ways to share your faith. Remember, you can find more resources, training and tools at greatcommissionalliance.org/evangelismresources and you can get many more ideas in my book 101 Easy, Effective, and Exciting Evangelism Ideas on Amazon.

ABOUT THE
CONTRIBUTORS

AUTHOR

Nate Herbst (Ph.D.) helps lead the Great Commission Alliance, a ministry that is committed to equipping believers everywhere for evangelism and discipleship. He is blessed to be joined in ministry by his wife Erin and together they have three wonderful children.

GRAPHIC DESIGN

Meghan Renfro, on staff with GCA, is passionate about serving Jesus and doing great graphic design for His glory. She is in full time ministry with her husband Ben, and their two sweet girls.

GCA
BOOKS AND RESOURCES

Get all of these incredible books and resources on Amazon.

 The BEST FACTS is our apologetics training tool. It is simple, easy to remember, comprehensive, and coherent.

 Following Jesus: Discipleship Essentials is our basic discipleship tool. Use this to help new believers grow in their faith and to equip believers for discipleship.

 Great Commission Leadership is our leadership training manual. It has 30 lessons and numerous appendices, which are full of great training and tools for evangelism and discipleship.

 101 Easy, Effective, and Exciting Evangelism Ideas is full of practical ideas for reaching virtually every corner of your sphere of influence.

ABOUT THE GCA

God is doing great things here at the Great Commission Alliance. Thousands of believers all across the globe are being mobilized for evangelism and discipleship.

OUR MISSION

Multiplying Christ-like Multipliers.

OUR VISION

The Great Commission Completed.

OUR STRATEGY

Intercession
Guidance
Next-generation ministry
International partnerships
Tools & technology
Equipping

WE WOULD BE HONORED TO HAVE YOU JOIN US IN THIS WORK

There are several exciting ways you can partner with us and the Lord in this ministry! You can do that by giving, going, and getting on your knees!

GIVING

This ministry is supported through the generosity of people like you. Visit **greatcommissionalliance.org/donate** to support this work. We would love to have you partner with us in all God is doing here!

GOING

The harvest is plentiful but the workers are few. We are always looking for new team members who will be willing to trust God and follow Him into a life of adventurous ministry. Contact us at **greatcommissionalliance.org/contact** if you would like to know more about what that could look like.

GETTING ON YOUR KNEES

We are so thankful for those that pray for us! We'll put you on our newsletter list if you send us a message at **greatcommissionalliance.org/contact.**

Made in the USA
San Bernardino, CA
24 May 2019